Walk Through The Valley

Walk Through The Valley

BY WILLIAM D.
LEIPOLD, Ph.D.

Library of Congress Catalog Card No. 74-21215

ISBN 0-8309-0137-X

Printed in the United States of America

Independence Press
Drawer HH
Independence, Missouri 64055

421   (1983-84)

Dedicated To

Val, John, David, and Bill
A small repayment for
many days absent.

Contents

Foreword   9

Author's Note 11

Acknowledgments 13

Chapter 1   You Too Could Be! 15

Chapter 2   Are You Rendered Helpless? 33

Chapter 3   Learning Behavior and Alcoholism . . . 40

Chapter 4   Conflicts (How We Handle Them) . . . 53

Chapter 5   What Protects Me (Defenses) 70

Chapter 6   Dynamics of Human Adjustment 86

Chapter 7   Creative Thinking (A Means to

                    Problem Solving) 99

Chapter 8   Responsibility 109

Chapter 9   Why Do I Have to Be Me? 118

Selected Bibliography 124

Foreword

Walk Through the Valley provides a special insight into alcoholism. Perhaps more importantly it provides an insight into each person's life, alcoholic or nonalcoholic. Dr. Leipold really alludes to this in his definition of an alcoholic—"a human being." Certainly we all share similar frustrations, tensions, fears, feelings of inadequacy and insecurity.

Dr. Leipold is unusually well qualified to probe the problem of alcoholism. His educational background and experiences in the field of alcoholism span two decades. He is former director of Heartview Foundation (alcoholism treatment center) in Mandan, North Dakota, and has been director of Valley Hope Alcoholism Treatment Center at Norton and Atchison, Kansas, since their origins in 1967.

As co-founder of Valley Hope, member of the Board of Directors, a family physician in Norton, Kansas, and part of the Valley Hope team (medical doctor), I have seen the concepts outlined in this book change the lives of people at Valley Hope.

I believe in the developing concept of the medical team approach, and particularly I believe in the special team approach to alcoholism as developed by Dr. Leipold. I have a great respect and admiration for him.

The book will appeal to the general public. It especially meets a need in the area of education for those attempting to help the alcoholic and his or her family—the physicians, ministers, social workers, psychologists, alcoholism counselors, law enforcement personnel, and others in the counseling field.

The big of Valley Hope is somewhat symbolic of our understanding of alcoholism. The circle around the emblem symbolizes the human being. The symbolizes social drinking. The downward slope of the is symbolic of alcoholism—problem drinking. The upward slope is symbolic of recovery or hope for the alcoholic.

Dr. Leipold and his staff at Valley Hope assume a basic trust in the individual as a human being (no locked doors) and challenge each patient to take responsibility for his own actions. As the alcoholic withdraws from family, friends, and associates to the solace offered by the bottle the problems multiply. The simple truth discovered at Valley Hope and portrayed in this book is that "people really do need people."

I found that once I had picked up the book I could not put it down until I had finished it. I predict that others will receive inspiration through new understanding.

Merlynn Colip, M.D.

Author's Note

Throughout my years of working in the field of alcoholism, I have seen a variety of methods for treating the alcoholic, some successful, some not. While the alcoholic has been seen by himself and by others as a strange breed of cat, I never could concur in that idea.

I define the alcoholic quite simply as a human being. The definition has played a major role in the treatment of the alcoholic at Valley Hope, for there we treat people—not different illnesses. I have written this book for people and it applies to all people, not just the alcoholic or those with related addictions.

People respond to love and concern. Love is the giving of one's self without expectation of reward. When we let someone know we care, and share ourselves with that person, there is a basis for recovery.

Many problems could be resolved if we could learn to accept people as they are rather than trying to mold them into something they are not. The same principle applies to our own self-acceptance. (It took me twenty-nine years to learn to like myself.) My years of experience, particularly those spent at Valley Hope, have enabled me to assemble a few helps to use in the daily business of living which I would like to share.

William D. Leipold, Ph.D.

Acknowledgments

To the members of my Board of Directors, a special thanks for the cooperation and encouragement given:

Judge Jean W. Kissell
LeRoy "Pete" Peterson
Guy L. Allen
Richard D. Boyd
George W. Wallace
Merlynn Colip, M.D.
E. F. Steichen, M.D.
Milton A. Nitsch
Mrs. Beatrice Williams
Tony Jewell
Mrs. Virginia Docking
Richard Kosman

Thanks also to Kay Knocke who was a big help in the early stages of the book—and to Gordy and Dennis for shouldering part of my load.

WDL

CHAPTER ONE

You Too Could Be!

The typical alcoholic who has come to Valley Hope may be from 4'9" to 6'8" tall; weigh between 72 and 270 pounds soaking wet; be male or female; have an I.Q. of anywhere between 67 and 143 and a completed education of from the third grade through a doctorate. He or she may be Methodist, Catholic, Jewish, Mormon, Presbyterian, Episcopalian, Lutheran, Buddhist, Hindu, Muslem, atheist, agnostic, or of any other faith; is married, widowed, divorced, or single; may be an unskilled laborer, lawyer, hod carrier, merchant, ditchdigger, teacher, truck driver, priest, plumber, doctor, janitor, policeman, or psychologist.

Anyone who drinks could be an alcoholic, but a more precise definition or description is needed. Marty Mann says it best when she describes an alcoholic as someone whose drinking causes a continuing or growing problem in any department in his life.* The alcoholic is, however, first and foremost

---

*To avoid clumsy sentence structure and repetition, the pronoun "he" is used for the most part in this book in referring to alcoholics. This is not meant to minimize the incidence of alcoholism among women nor to assign it lesser importance.

a person, a human being with thoughts and feelings. I like Marty Mann's definition because it doesn't center around the consumption of alcohol but rather highlights the fact that this person whom we label alcoholic has problems. The alcoholic will deny the alcoholism (in fact, in a Valley Hope study it was determined that this denial caused the alcoholic an extra 13.5 years of drinking), but the alcoholic has difficulty denying that he has marital, financial, family, or legal problems.

Working in the field of alcoholism I learned quickly that an alcoholic will deny (and often to an early death) that he is alcoholic. A young man who is now recovering wrote to me about his failure to recognize his own alcoholism:

> Television was a fascinating companion in my drinking days. Often, I would come out of an alcoholic blackout and find myself thoroughly engrossed in watching a test pattern!
>
> I remember one particular program vividly. The "Days of Wine and Roses" was shown one night and I watched it to see just what an alcoholic was. (As you know, by this time in my life, Doctor, I had been married three times to two women, was in jeopardy of losing another marriage, had worked out a method of drinking so that I was drunk usually three times a day, and had been experiencing blackouts for six years!)
>
> I remember that the star of the show was recovering from his alcoholism in Alcoholics Anonymous and was trying to persuade his practicing alcoholic wife to try sobriety. Evidently the confrontation was too threatening to her, and

she turned again to the bottle. Her absurd behavior in refusing this last chance for sobriety and a reunion with her family brought forth a seething rage from me. Whisky glass in hand, I shouted at the screen. Couldn't she see that she was missing her last chance? Presently, though, I consoled myself by drinking into oblivion. I knew perfectly well *she* was alcoholic, but *I* had no problems.

The dictionary defines alcoholism as a tendency to the excessive use of alcohol. It also describes an alcoholic as one with a personality disorder, the most prominent symptom of which is chronic, compulsive drinking.

Let's examine the definitions more closely. We would agree that one with "a personality disorder" has something wrong with his personality. Some might say the person was "odd," "peculiar," or even "nuts." "Abnormal" might be a more accurate term—at least it indicates that the person has a problem. A "symptom" is a danger signal. Similar to a high fever, it indicates something is wrong. It doesn't tell us what, but it says, "Get going and find out what's happening." In this definition, the symptom is "chronic, compulsive drinking." In other words, the alcoholic has a dual problem: (1) his problem drinking, and (2) the etiology or reason why he drinks. In interviewing hundreds of alcoholics, I have never encountered one who drinks to excess because it's fun. The excessive drinking is the result of a problem manifesting itself in the life of the alcoholic.

In the book *A.A. Comes of Age,* we read: "Put those two things together—a world living under the domination of fear and a world filled with alcohol and with alcoholic suggestion—and you can see how important it is that people realize what alcoholism really is: a deep-seated emotional illness that must be treated according to psychosomatic principles. Psychosomatic, of course, simply means body and soul."

In "The Big Book" this concept is further explained: "Though our decision was a vital and crucial step, it could have little permanent effect unless at once followed by a strenuous effort to face, and to be rid of, the things in ourselves which had been blocking us. Our liquor was but a symptom. So we had to get down to causes and conditions.... The main problem of the alcoholic centers in his mind, rather than in his body."

Many alcoholics and some alcoholism programs have difficulty with this concept. As long as a distinction is made between treating the person and treating the alcohol, the alcoholic will not be helped. In my opinion the success of Alcoholics Anonymous is based upon an understanding of this concept. The treatment of the total person is beautifully locked up in the Twelve Steps and Twelve Traditions of A. A. Alcoholics Anonymous sees the humanness of the alcoholic and launches a recovery program with the *person* the No. 1 att   tion.

Literally, all the home remedies people use to force a recovery program are aimed at alcohol rather than at the alcoholic. These run the gamut from pouring out the booze to telling the person, "All you have to do is stop drinking. Use some willpower." The key is to look a little deeper and to try to understand what is motivating the person to use the chemical to such a degree in the first place. E. M. Jellinek stated the case quite well when he said, "Alcoholism may be the source of much human misery...but fundamentally, human misery is the source of alcoholism."

The alcoholic has great difficulty in thinking of himself as "nuts" (abnormal). Yet it is enlightening to listen to him tell about his exploits, both drunk and sober.

An alcoholic recently treated indicated that for eleven years he had experienced a major problem with his wife. She always poured his glass of milk before setting the food on the table; consequently when it was time to eat, his milk was "warm." This made him angry, but the problem persisted for eleven years. One day his counselor asked him to confront his wife with the warm milk problem. The usual excuses were forthcoming—"...want to avoid an argument," "...don't want to hurt her because she's such a wonderful person," and so on. At any rate, the counselor's advice prevailed, and the alcoholic returned home to work up his courage. He stated to his wife in no uncertain terms that after eleven years of warm milk, he wanted cold milk for supper. His spouse's reply was one word, "Fine." Our alcoholic friend had allowed a problem to work on him that didn't even exist as far as his spouse was concerned.

Another alcoholic who exhibited odd behavior dressed up in his best suit, started drinking, went for a drive, and ended up sitting in pouring rain in a field of tomatoes, deliriously tasting one after another.

A recovering alcoholic who was editor of a suburban newspaper in the early fifties when much of the Midwest experienced severe floods told one of his experiences. At that time in his life his drinking was at a high. One day, after waking up from a two-week binge, he decided to go out for another bottle. As he left his house he noticed that the entire town was deserted. National Guard troops immediately surrounded him and wanted to know what he was doing in the street. The town had been evacuated, the flood had come and gone, and he, the editor of the newspaper, knew nothing about it.

The "insane" things which happen to an alcoholic as a result of drinking aren't always as dramatic as these, but the stories are endless.

Alcoholism has been defined by experts in the field as an addiction process. Addiction is simply a need out of control. Suppose a person is suffering from one character defect, inferiority. He finds out through experience that three or four drinks will help restore his capacity to talk. He will continue or repeat the use of alcohol to facilitate conversation as long as it does the job.

During lectures at the treatment center we ask, "How many of you converse better after three or four drinks?" About 70 percent reply affirmatively. The sedative chemical alcohol, like a Band-Aid, covers up the feeling of inferiority for a period of time, allowing the user to see himself as "normal." The need to achieve acceptance and normality cries out for response.

How does this need get out of control? People are motivated by pleasure. The choices made and the actions taken are motivated by pleasure. The utilization of the beverage alcohol allows the individual to hide his inadequacies and to fulfill his need for self-expression. Worthwhile activities may be abandoned because they induce pain, and escape from pain is pleasurable.

Alcohol itself is a sedative drug, not a stimulant as the majority of lay people think. Because it is a sedative, when taken in certain quantities it produces pleasurable results. If the individual is operating under some type of tension when he takes alcohol, that drug will reduce the tension. Once the tension is reduced, the person reports to himself a feeling of well-being, and it is this feeling that he wants to repeat with the continued use of the beverage.

Tension + **= Reduced Tension**

In any conversation concerning alcohol, the word "need" is usually heard often. The businessman comes home and says, "Honey, fix me a couple of martinis; I need a drink." He is really saying, "I am tense, I want to experience a feeling of well-being," so he turns to the sedative chemical alcohol. This man is drinking for the effect that particular beverage gives him. It is at this point that there should be concern about the possibility of addiction.

Initially and quite often through the chronic stages, alcohol helps produce pleasurable feelings in an individual.

Alcohol is a chemical. Because it is, it has a position on the chemical danger scale. At the bottom of the scale are food and water; at the top, the deadly poisons. Alcohol fits somewhere in the middle. There are certain things we have to know about any chemical in order to determine the degree of harm it might cause. We must know its position on the scale, and consider the dosage—how much and how often we take it. The third criterion is the resistance of the individual to it.

1. Position

2. Dosage:

   How much?
   How often?

3. Resistance of individual to the chemical.

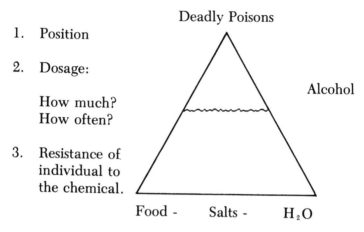

Deadly Poisons

Alcohol

Food -   Salts - H_2O

When I was chief psychologist at a state hospital, our medical doctors gave a drug called curare to patients prior to electric shock treatment. Curare is a deadly poison which can stop the respiratory system. How did they get by with its use? They knew it was a poison, they knew how much to give, and through research they knew the resistance each patient had to it. Instead of killing, it functioned as a relaxant and could be used appropriately.

As long as a chemical is used with these precautions it seldom hurts anyone. Unfortunately, human beings choose to self-prescribe. It's almost as if they determine that if one dose does such a good job, two will do even better.

If one is given a medicine to use at 8:00, 12:00, 4:00, and 8:00 and takes it as prescribed at 8:00 and 12:00, forgets 4:00, and then takes two doses at 8:00, he is a chemical misuser. The doctor is prescribing a continual flow of the chemical through the system, but the patient interrupts it at one point and doubles it at another.

Self-prescription increases alcoholic or drug addiction processes. Anything taken in excess becomes a detriment to the human system. As a general rule, the greater the stress the individual is operating under, the greater the dose needed to quiet the stress. If the alcoholic is operating under a great deal of tension, a greater amount of alcohol is needed to relieve it than if the tension is minor. The alcoholic is in a self-medicated anxiety state for whom inebriation is an unfortunate coincidence of tension reduction. He may have an excellent doctor (himself), but he has a fool for a patient.

There are probably as many types of addictions as there are people. Society, however, determines the gradations of "goodness" or "Godness" in an addiction.

Let's look at six addictions—alcohol, gambling, drugs, smoking, food, and work. These are all quite similar in their symptomatologies. Before we go on, it is important that we understand two concepts: (1) a person does not have to have a psychological disorder or problem to initiate an addiction process, and (2) no chemical is dangerous unless taken in excess.

ALCOHOL

In today's so-called enlightened age the alcoholic is supposedly seen as a "sick" individual. I think many say this but don't really believe it. Understanding is greater, but the majority of people still consider the alcoholic to be a "drunken bum," and believe all he really needs to do is stop drinking.

Imagine that we are attending the funeral of a practicing alcoholic. The minister is hard-pressed to say anything good about the deceased. He seeks solace for the family, not by eulogizing the dead but by reading from the word of God. It is most difficult to praise a practicing alcoholic.

GAMBLING

The gambling addict is not necessarily considered a sick person by society. People may say, "That dirty so-and-so spends all his family's food money on a card game," but they don't consider the individual to be ill.

An example of the depth of the sickness of a gambling addict is the man I had in treatment once who carried two bags of washers of equal value with him. He would wake up in the middle of the night in a sweat, get up, and gamble against himself with the two bags of washers as stakes until one side beat the other. Then he could go back to sleep.

The funeral of a gambling addict is also a difficult one for the minister.

DRUGS

A drug addict in our society is seen as a sick person. When a death occurs people say, "Isn't it a shame...it's such a waste that one so young had to die in such a foolish way."

The symptomatology of drug addiction is similar to alcohol addiction. Regardless of the attention other drug addictions get, alcohol still remains the No. 1 drug problem in the United States.

The minister at a funeral of a drug addict has no difficulty in finding much to say about such a senseless, useless, and great tragedy.

SMOKING

The smoking addict today is caught "between the devil and the deep blue sea." Pressure is being exerted on him. He is beginning to feel the stigma of being an individual who lacks willpower. Does that sound familiar? It's almost exactly what society has said about the user of alcohol. It wouldn't surprise me to see clinics open soon for the smoker similar to those operating today for the alcoholic.

Smokers are seen as weak people without the guts to quit, particularly when they know that smoking produces emphysema and cancer and that they will lose 8.3 years of life while they continue to use the "cancer stick." Still, when the funeral is over and the pallbearers are lighting up their cigarettes on the way to the graveyard, there are generally good feelings toward and comments about the deceased.

FOOD

According to recent statistics, 50 percent of the U.S. population is overweight. The pattern of a food addict is almost identical to that of an alcoholic.

When does the food addict go to the refrigerator, when the room is full of people or when it is empty? He or she will hide food just as the alcoholic hides the bottle. A heavy person will often lie about the actual amount of food consumed, and use the excuse, "All I have to do is look at food and I gain three pounds."

I went to a TOPS Club meeting and presented the 44 symptoms of alcoholism. I left out the word "alcohol" in the discussion, and talked only in terms of the symptoms. About three-fourths of the way through the meeting, a gal who was wearing a pair of slacks big enough for two people stood up and said, "Doctor, you're talking about me."

Society is much kinder to the food addict than to the alcoholic. If a food addict dies on the operating table because the surgeon couldn't get down through the blubber to the vital organs, he will have a good funeral. The eight pallbearers who accompany him to the graveyard because six couldn't carry the casket will tell about the wonderful guy he was, jolly, always happy. Many beautiful things will be said about him.

WORK

The one addict I consider the sickest of all is the work addict. He's the one, in terms of our culture, who is the most wonderful person in town. He will do anything you want him to do at any time under any given circumstance. This is the man who works twelve, fourteen, sixteen, or eighteen hours a day. He's the one who leads the drives and heads the committees. The townspeople all know who he is and won't hesitate to tell you what a wonderful person he is.

Interestingly enough statistics show that the work addict dies somewhere between the ages of 47 and 55. This is also true of the alcoholic.

When the work addict dies from exhaustion and the funeral is held, the minister will have to quit eulogizing after two and one-half hours because his throat hurts. He could go on for another two or three hours about what a wonderful guy the deceased was.

However, if you file by the coffin and are listening, you will hear his children say, "Mom, who is that man?" If you had asked the work addict why he was working so hard he would certainly have told you it was for his family. He got up and went to work at six in the morning and didn't get home until eleven at night. The children went to bed at ten at night and woke up at seven; they never knew the man.

The work addict is probably one of the most selfish people in the world, not excepting the alcoholic who is also a very selfish person. The work addict must work the way he does to achieve ego gratification. He does it for the "pat on the back." He can't find this within himself. He lacks security.

The reason I say the work addict is worse off than the alcoholic is that he receives only positive rewards for his behavior. The alcoholic usually will get into enough trouble with his drinking that he or someone else will finally do something about the problem. When the work addict receives nothing but rewards from others for his behavior he will continue that behavior.

Much of what happens in the addictive process is dependent on how society views the addiction. If it is considered bad, then such a label is attached and the addict is inclined to try to avoid that stigma. If the addiction is viewed as good, however, society not only issues a stamp of approval but positively reinforces the behavior pattern.

If one is going to have an addiction, it is better to have one which creates pain either for self or for others than to have one which is pleasurable. At least in pain there is hope for recovery in which the person can find his or her real self.

THE TOTAL PERSON

Generally speaking, a person's personality is the sum of what he is. In treatment, the total person must be helped. One of the more effective ways to aid the alcoholic is to consider him from the psychological, social, medical, and spiritual aspects of his life.

Some professionals treat only the medical needs of the alcoholic. They spend considerable time in the withdrawal process, possibly place the patient on drugs in an effort to help, and then send him or her home. Shortly, the patient is back for a return engagement. The alcohol was successfully treated but not the alcoholic.

To treat the alcoholic one must help the total person. The initial stage of alcoholism takes from five to twenty-five years to develop before moving into the acquired stage. From the outset the sedative effects of the beverage alcohol produce a pleasurable or euphoric effect on the drinker. Not only does the alcoholic feel that he converses better after the drinking of an alcoholic beverage but does a better job of dancing, skating, singing, etc. What the person is really saying is, "I don't think I can do these things adequately without the boost given me by the beverage alcohol." Ask any alcoholic to think back to the mild stages of alcoholism and he or she will usually report that drinking produced fun.

From a medical standpoint it is known that the very first drink marks the beginning of interference with the body organs. Some studies indicate brain damage occurs with every drink a human being takes. The good Lord made us in such a way that often we can abuse ourselves extensively before it shows up. but sooner or later, excessive quantities of alcohol taken into the body will produce visible brain damage as well as other physical problems.

Initial State—During the initial stage of alcoholism which constitutes the more problemless area of the alcoholic's life, the individual has few apparent problems. The drinking has not yet caused family, friends, or neighbors to notice that it has gone beyond "social" drinking. Yet the beginnings of alcoholism are quite evident.

Acquired Stage—The acquired stage of alcoholism is reached when the alcoholic simply acquires a psychological and physiological dependence on alcohol. As soon as Fred is told by his wife, mother, or friend that he drinks too much, he's in trouble. Once he moves into the acquired stage, there apparently is no return. Once he goes beyond that invisible line, the only known "cure" for him is abstinence.

To meet the psychological needs of the acquired stage alcoholics begin to develop an elaborate alibi system. They are superb con artists, and in essence, they have to be. Their strategy pattern is to make the person who is threatening their drinking believe that they are able to handle the drinking, or they may project on to that person responsibility for their drinking. This is one reason why spouses of alcoholics are tabbed as "dumb," "stupid," and "ignorant." Talk to a spouse and invariably he or she will tell you of attacks by the alcoholic on his or her character. In order for alcoholics to justify their drinking they must do this.

After alcoholics have moved into the acquired stage, the social and spiritual areas of their lives begin to suffer. They alienate themselves from the church. Friends, family, and the job may begin to interfere with their drinking and therefore have to be eliminated. So they move farther and farther away from people, away from any power greater than themselves. They view themselves and their ever present bottle as having absolute control over their behavior.

In the acquired stage there are more evidences of medical problems—hand tremors, DTs, brain and liver damage. The stupidity of alcoholism is evidenced by the fact that one's hands will shake because of the excessive use of alcohol, yet the alcoholics will reach for a drink to stop the tremors. They use the problem to try to effect a cure.

As diseases go, alcoholism may not be too bad to have. At least there is something that can be done about it if the individual is willing to look for help. Recovery can be made psychologically, medically, socially, and spiritually.

The psychological problems—the alibis, the lying, cheating, and hiding of the bottle—can be handled if approached properly. I'm not suggesting that all an alcoholic's psychological problems will be solved, for they will not be, but if the alcoholic wants to put some effort into it, he can deal with many of them.

The social and spiritual problems can also be treated. An individual can get involved again with church, friends, and family. Some of the deepest friendships are cultivated while in treatment or through A.A. There is usually a job available if the alcoholic will take it although it may not be as president of a company. Most employers are supportive if the alcoholic does something about the problem. The community too, in spite of what most alcoholics think, quite often is thrilled when a man or woman achieves sobriety.

Medically speaking, if a person has been a chronic drinker and has brain damage, nothing can be done to restore the damaged areas. However, it is possible to activate other portions of the brain through retraining to assume some of the functions of the damaged cells. Most of the other medical problems the individual may have encountered as a result of drinking can be treated, including the damaged liver which can usually still be made to function.

There are nine million alcoholics in the United States, and there are only 450,000 in A.A. What happens to the others? In general there are four ways the alcoholic surrenders to alcohol. In spite of the great amount of information available about alcoholism, the majority of alcoholics go to the grave without benefit of treatment. Their disease-induced deaths may be recorded as heart attacks, cirrhosis of the liver, or other ailments.

A second method of surrendering is suicide. When one becomes aware of the feelings of worthlessness and understands the loneliness the alcoholic faces, one can see that to the alcoholic suicide is a feasible solution to the problem.

Complete surrender to alcohol in the "skid row" level of response is the situation of only 3 percent of the alcoholic population. However, in one sense all of the people who die without help have surrendered to alcohol. Alcoholics are slaves. As long as they continue to drink, the bottle will tell them what to do. They essentially say to John Barleycorn, "O Lord and Master, I will do as you direct." This includes selling one's coat in the middle of a Minnesota winter for a gallon of wine. No practicing alcoholic is free; alcohol will tell him or her what to do, how to do it, and when to do it.

A fourth level of surrender is to obtain treatment. There are any number of places to receive aid—A.A., treatment centers both private and public, churches, hospitals, or even jail. The type of treatment doesn't matter as long as it works and the individual finds sobriety as a way of life. The difficulty for the alcoholic comes in acceptance of treatment and realization that before recovery is possible there must be unconditional surrender. The alcoholic is asked to give up a way of life that for many years has sustained him in the face of stress. The concept of unconditional surrender leaves him feeling helpless. His resistance is understandable.

I have never had an alcoholic come running up the Valley Hope driveway with arms outstretched shouting, "Here I am, help me." To the alcoholic treatment is not that desirable, yet one who ends up in treatment is very lucky regardless of how he or she got there. Those who assume responsibility for getting alcoholics into treatment have to have a great deal of love and they have undoubtedly already shared a great deal of hurt. It is no easy thing to see a loved one become frightened, dependent, and miserable. Alcohol has been the coping mechanism; now through treatment the alcoholic is asked to relinquish the one thing that makes life tolerable. No wonder that person feels helpless and afraid.

CHAPTER TWO

Are You Rendered Helpless?

How would you like someone to walk up and say to you, "You're unable to help yourself; you're dependent, feeble, incompetent, incapable, and without recourse to help"? I'd rather want to lean back and plant one fist on that someone's big mouth. I wouldn't care to hear that about myself or for that matter about anyone else. Yet this describes the situation of the alcoholic. The inability to cope renders him helpless. This, in turn, creates the motivation to seek that which he feels will restore him to "normalcy." He wants to feel good and his behavior is directed toward achieving that end.

There are those who feel that the alcoholic's behavior indicates a wish for self-destruction. When one learns what an alcoholic does to himself it is easy to agree. This may also be true of other types of illnesses, particularly emotional or mental illness. At least in those cases it's the person suffering from the disease who receives the major brunt of the pain. With alcoholism many people suffer. To the alcoholic there is physical destruction to the brain and liver as well as general deterioration. There is also increased lack of emotional control evidenced by unsound or inappropriate behavior. The fact that there is economic destruction is obvious with others sharing the consequences. Destruction of the alcoholic's social life is seen in the loss of friends and rejection by family. Any spiritual life he may have had is destroyed by the failure to recognize any power greater than himself. In spite of all this the practicing alcoholic drinks to live and lives to drink.

When the alcoholic enters treatment and the "fog" lifts he won't deny these destructive tendencies. He may have a hundred excuses for them but he does admit they are present. He can feel them, he can see them. Why would individuals want to place themselves on such a road to self-destruction?

The emotion that manifests itself most prominently in self-destructive behavior is anger. You don't destroy when you are happy; you destroy when you are angry. This includes self-destruction or suicide. The person who kills himself has to be angry at himself. Anger leads to destruction, and inability to cope with oneself and/or one's environment (helplessness) leads to anger—anger at oneself and/or others.

Anger takes many forms; one of the obvious forms of anger is rage. Blane defines an alcoholic as a person in a *chronic* state of rage. Now most of us don't live our lives in a chronic state of anger and neither does the alcoholic. However if one looks beneath the facade created by the alcoholic there is a definite feeling of lack of personal worth. Most alcoholics entering treatment at Valley Hope feel most comfortable when they can say negative things about themselves. If we try to indicate to them early in treatment that they have positive values as well as negative ones, we meet resistance.

Loss of a sense of personal worth is usually reflected in behavior we call depression. Rage is externalized anger. Think of the last time you were "down in the dumps." What were your thoughts, what were your actions? Were they positively or negatively directed? I'll bet you thought very negative thoughts concerning yourself.

Many synonyms can be found for the word "anger," including resentment, jealousy, envy, and hostility. Anger leads to destruction but it is our inability to handle our lives that leads to feelings of anger. When we feel helpless and are exposed we very quickly revert to anger. The symptoms of helplessness are easy to describe—inner feelings of uncertainty, impending doom, things aren't just right, and waiting for an explosion. Worry, fear, tensions, anxieties are all present symptoms.

Anxiety is a nondirected fear while fear itself is direct. For example, if a lion walked into your room you would experience fear; you would know what the danger was. However, if the door blew open and weird noises were heard, the feelings you would experience would be anxious feelings. You wouldn't actually know what was happening.

The spouse of the alcoholic can tell you about anxiety and feelings of helplessness, particularly when she knows the man she loves is drinking but she doesn't know where or how much. Ask her what it feels like at 3:00 a.m. when she is waiting for her alcoholic husband to arrive home. You might also ask her about the feelings of anger building up as each tension-producing minute goes by.

TENSION→FEELINGS OF HELPLESSNESS→ ANGRY BEHAVIOR→NEGATIVE THOUGHTS

When the husband doesn't come home a feeling of helplessness is produced resulting in many angry thoughts about what she will do when he does get home. He will face an angry person upon his arrival.

When he runs up against an obstacle the alcoholic handles his tension a little differently. Supposing Joe receives a promotion that Fred feels he should have had. Fred cannot attack his boss, but the frustrated feelings inside about not obtaining the promotion himself causes him to resort to detrimental behavior. I know of a "Fred" who was bypassed for promotion who took a two-week trip abroad. He drank so heavily while he was there that he realized he had taken the trip only when the bills began coming in.

We put ourselves in positions with which we cannot cope and then have to find ways to deal with the resulting helplessness. Alcoholism is such coping behavior. Under its influence we can "be what we want and do what we want." Alcohol will cover up many unpleasant feelings.

While the utilization of alcohol will eventually lead to self-destruction, one of the paradoxes of alcoholism is that for a period of time alcohol will slow down the self-destructive behavior. People drink for effect. The sedative nature of alcohol reduces the tension of living and for a period of time allows one to reduce his negative thoughts. Drinking allows one to feel power, power not felt without the drink. Fred sits in a bar wanting to call his wife to tell her he will be late. After three-plus drinks Fred can call Mary and inform her in no uncertain terms that he will be as late as he pleases. Fred has successfully counteracted his fear of calling by applying his alcohol Band-Aid.

If alcohol is one's only release valve, serious difficulty results, for it will soon become a problem within a problem. It is most difficult for one to admit he is helpless, admit that he cannot cope with his world as it exists for him. No one wants others to know he is "weak" so he works overtime to compensate for any such feelings.

Alcohol reduces the feelings of helplessness. It covers them up and for the period of time that alcohol is in one's system he is a "new person."

Part of the treatment of alcoholism is to remove the helplessness, to allow the alcoholic to depend on himself and others to handle his problems, not the alcohol. A.A. does this beautifully. The following is the first of A.A.'s Twelve Steps: "We admitted we were powerless over alcohol—that our lives had become unmanageable." Admitting and accepting powerlessness over something that can't be handled (helplessness) gives one the "power" to remove the helpless feeling. What a relief it must be for the alcoholic to accept the fact that alcohol whips him, for he can then adapt a program of action to help him overcome his helplessness. The next eleven steps of the A.A. program lead him out of his helpless state and carry him into a sharing and caring state in which he can finally give of himself to others.

The key concept in stopping helplessness is to become involved with others. This is the beautiful message of A.A. When the alcoholic can find the "guts" to ask for help for his helplessness he is on the road to recovery.

Helplessness comes from many sources and the feelings of helplessness may be given many other names. The literature on alcoholism abounds with these names. Alcoholics are said to be perfectionistic and compulsive people. A perfectionist is a person who wants things just right. But this person can never get things sufficiently right. He who is always trying to reach too high keeps himself in a chronic state of helplessness. Take for example the thirty-one-year-old alcoholic who told himself that he had to have $200,000 saved by the time he was forty. There was no way this could be done. Consequently he had perpetual feelings of helplessness. (See case history on this man in "Dynamics of Human Adjustment" chapter.)

The "Peter Principle" is an excellent evaluation of human behavior. It simply states that in a hierarchy all people will tend to rise to their level of incompetency. All keep striving until a level of helplessness is reached. People also tend to rise to their level of *emotional incompetence;* they keep adding stress until the stress itself is unmanageable.

Another word signifying helplessness is dependency. The dependent personality must rely on others to make his decisions. Blane's book *Personality of the Alcoholic—Guises of Dependency* illustrates quite graphically the nature of dependency in alcoholism.

I believe that the alcoholic is a dependent person who, contrary to his personality, tries to assert his independence. It's basically the same conflict we see in teen-agers. Any unresolved conflict leaves a feeling of helplessness. If one can find something that not only appears to allow him to make decisions but gives him the "power" to do so, then certainly he is going to make use of that even though it leads to self-destruction. That is the dilemma of alcoholism.

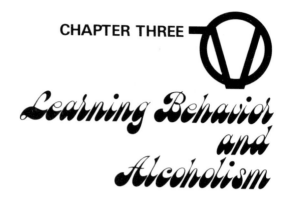

CHAPTER THREE

Learning Behavior and Alcoholism

If you had all the knowledge in the world, it would be worthless unless you could use what you had. Learning is acquired knowledge plus performance. It is the utilization of what God has given you, heredity, and the combination of this with the environment which, in turn, formed you.

Let's assume for the moment that we have an infant who is hungry. Hunger is a tension producer. It places the infant in unpleasant circumstances, and therefore initiates a response. The major response of an infant to a tension-producing situation such as hunger is to cry. This produces tension in the mother initiating a response which results in taking care of the need of the child. Mother comes in, feeds the child, and the usual response to the satisfaction of hunger reduction is sleep. In this way the infant reports its happiness with the situation.

Any time a person is under tension there will be some type of response from that individual. The response from the child was crying which created tension in the mother. This tension was pain producing to her also and to reduce this she responded by feeding the child. Then the infant reported to the mother that everything was wonderful by his behavior—sleep. The mother experienced the feeling that everything was wonderful, too. She experienced satisfaction. There are two types of tension operating here: the child's is basically physical while the mother's is emotional.

The primary reward the child received was food which reduced the physiological tension. But there were also secondary rewards. If while providing the food the mother holds the child properly, there is warmth; she may talk to the baby softly; she may pat it gently. These are all secondary reinforcements operating off the primary one which is food, and they operate in terms of the emotional component of that child who is learning love, security, and the feeling of being adequate.

Let us look at the concept of reward. If the reward is a pleasurable one based on the feeling of the person receiving it, then all other aspects associated with that reward will be pleasurable. The child received love and warmth associated with hunger reduction and reported the outcome in satisfied sleep.

Rewards differ for different people. What pleases you wouldn't necessarily please me. There is a story told of a white man who saved the life of a tribal chief (Whaley and Malott). The chief wanted to reward this man so he gave him his most treasured possession, his No. 1 wife, who happened to be old, fat, and toothless. There was an immediate reaction on the part of the white man whose value system was different than the chief's, and he turned the gift down. To have a positive reward value, the reward must be meaningful to the person receiving it.

SKINNER BOX

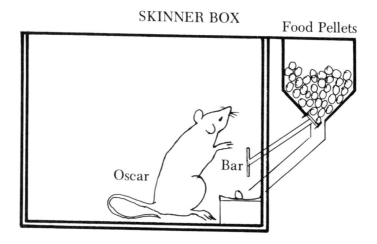

Let me introduce you to Oscar. Oscar is a naïve white rat. What is a rat doing in a book on alcoholism? Well, I've been told that alcoholics have been called many things and perhaps "rat" has been among them. At any rate I'd like you to become acquainted with him, for hopefully he is going to teach us some of the principles of learning. We will put Oscar, twenty-four hours hungry, into a box designed by B. F. Skinner for use in learning experiments. Within the box is a bar placed just above a tray into which food pellets fall when the bar is pressed. The food pellets are located in another box which is elevated and rigged to release the pellets as the bar is pressed. We have put Oscar into the box hungry in order to increase the motivation; this is the same situation as trying to motivate the alcoholic to want help.

We are going to teach the rat a new behavior, something he has never done. What we want to teach him is to press the bar down. He will run around the cage and eventually press the bar which releases a food pellet. The pellet is a primary reward that helps reduce the tension from hunger. It is a positive reward. Because one pellet will not relieve the hunger Oscar will continue to search for ways of finding food. Because the food is a positive reward, Oscar will eventually "learn" that there is a connection between the pressing of the bar and the resulting reward of food. He will continue to press the bar until his hunger has been satisfied. Oscar is receiving 100 percent reinforcement: for every one unit of work, he gets one unit of reward (1_w-1_r).

One man, Guthrie, says we operate on one-trial learning. He claims that the rat actually learned all this with one reinforcement, one pellet of food. The subsequent food pellets strengthened Oscar's bar pressing behavior.

Now we can take the rat out and have him go another twenty-four hours without food. If we put him back in the box after that time, he will begin bar pressing again because of the motivational force of hunger (pain). He will try to reduce the pain.

We have taught Oscar a certain form of behavior and now would like to set this behavior so that the chances of it changing will be minimal. We will change the reinforcement schedule to require ten units of work for one unit of reward. He will have to press the bar ten times to obtain one pellet of food. We'll find that once this is learned, Oscar will work harder for the same amount of reward. The reduction of hunger tension is still the motivating force for Oscar's behavior. This is simply a fixed schedule of reward. Many workers are rewarded for their labor within this type of framework.

Perhaps a much better reward system however is the interval type. We will now reward Oscar based on variable numbers of bar presses. What Oscar should learn is that if he continues to press the bar sooner or later he will receive the reward. Oscar doesn't know when it will happen but he does learn that if he continues the behavior, the reward will come.

This is similar to people playing a slot machine. Any person with average intelligence knows that slot machines are "fixed" to provide the house with the winning percentage. If he knows that playing a slot machine over a period of time he must lose, then why play? Why would anyone be so "dumb" as to play a machine when he knows he will lose? The answer lies in reinforcement theory.

The player puts his nickel in the slot, presses the bar, and a whirring noise starts. Pictures of various fruits line up before him, and if the fruits line up in a predetermined method, the player receives a reinforcement. By the way, the player is positively reinforced simply by playing the machine; however, it's when those nickels drop that the feeling of goodness arrives and the player can be said to be "hooked."

I watched a woman in Las Vegas who was playing the quarter machine. She hit the jackpot, and the quarters came pouring out; she jumped up and down, clapped her hands, and the machine lights were flashing and the bells were ringing. The pit boss came over and loudly proclaimed, "Another jackpot." These were all positive reinforcements for the player which are designed to get the player to continue feeding the machine.

When the place settled down and she started putting quarters back in the machine, I asked her how much she had won. The jackpot was $125 and the nearest she could guess that she had put in was approximately $300 over a period of several days. And yet she was ecstatic over "winning" the jackpot.

Oscar has learned the same thing as the person on the slot machine; sooner or later the cherries will come up and the quarters will drop.

In a further attempt to observe Oscar's behavior, we decide to change his bar pressing action. The fastest way to do so is to stop the reinforcement—in this case, stop feeding Oscar. Now Oscar has been taught that if he presses the bar he will be fed. When he presses the bar now, he will not be fed. This is rather like the man who works for $200 a week and is told that now he can be paid only $25 for his work. When Oscar no longer receives the food, he stops bar pressing. How about the $200 a week worker; do you think he will continue to work?

Behavior on a 100 percent reinforcement schedule is easy to stop. Most of the time removing the positive reinforcer will do the trick.

According to the $(10_w\text{-}1_r)$ schedule before Oscar finds out he's not going to get the reward, he has to do ten units of work. This means that stopping the behavior by removing the reward will take a little longer, but Oscar will eventually stop working. It is the same with the variable interval reinforcement.

What happens if you take away the food or inflict punishment under the interval reward system? Oscar will work for you until the pain becomes greater than the anticipation of reward. Oscar has been taught, as many human beings are taught, to try one more time. "If I put one more quarter in the slot, I'll get the jackpot, and just as sure as I stop someone else will come along and win." This behavior will continue until the pain of the work overcomes the pain of the hunger or whatever is causing the problem.

What do Oscar and the slot machine have to do with alcoholism? Let us take a closer look at the three stages of alcoholism: mild, moderate, and chronic.

In the mild stage of alcoholism, the majority of alcoholics will report that with the ingestion of alcohol the result was "fun." The alcoholic will say upon thinking back that in the early stages of his drinking he enjoyed living, and alcohol was a part of that enjoyment. Basically, each time he drank he received a positive reinforcement from his drinking (a good time). This is similar to 100 percent reinforcement. With this type of reinforcement the alcoholic continues to drink, still receiving pleasure in association with drinking.

As the drinking increases he begins to create problems for others in his life. Thus a loved one might say, "Fred, you drink too much." By this time in the progression of the illness, Fred has entered the moderate stage of drinking. He is now receiving something he really doesn't want—punishment— because his behavior is now part of the overall picture. The punishment, however, is inflicted by others, not by Fred who for the most part is still receiving positive rewards for his behavior.

Basically, in the moderate stage he will go to a party and everything will be positive. He then will go to another party where he stands on the table with a lampshade on his head, turning himself on and off. We might say he makes a fool of himself. This is not necessarily true. What has happened is that Fred has made a fool of whoever accompanied him to that party. Fred is not hurting, but his spouse is. His spouse later confronts him with his behavior, and thus Fred's punishment from his drinking comes not necessarily from the drinking but from his spouse who resents his behavior.

Fred's reinforcement is still positive; his problem now centers around the negative reinforcement his behavior is giving to others. Once Fred has been confronted, the behavior changes—not the drinking but his behavior. He begins to do the things that strongly identify the alcoholic—lying about amount, hiding bottles, resenting his wife. It's the spouse that wants him to stop drinking, not Fred. It's the spouse who is hurting, not Fred, and it's the spouse's insistence that Fred stop drinking that changes his behavior. Thus appears the beautiful alibi system of the alcoholic. Assuming the alcoholic drinks to reduce tension, the position of the spouse increases tension and then the drinking is increased and the alcoholic moves along to the chronic stage of alcoholism. Here it looks as if the reinforcement theory goes down the drain.

There is an excessive punishment that the chronic alcoholic goes through. The loss of job, family, church, community, and, above all, the loss of self-respect are all part of this. Then why does this person continue to drink in the face of sheer disaster? Basically, under this theory and with the apparent punishment that the chronic alcoholic is taking, one would expect his behavior to "stop." In other words, we would normally expect the alcoholic to give up alcohol.

Let's look at his punishment. For the most part, from the moderate to the early chronic stages, the punishment received by the alcoholic has come as a result of the hurt of others. Because the spouse hurts, she has been inflicting pain on Fred, such as making countless threats, pouring booze down the drain, going home to mother. Most pressures on Fred are external to him—job, church, community. But what about Fred? Alcohol is a sedative chemical regardless of whether it's used in the mild or chronic stages of drinking. Because it is a sedative, the ingestion of it is still going to produce the desired result. True, when he's on it, he's catching "hell" from all sides, but as long as his old buddy John Barleycorn is inside him the sedative effects will work to reduce the pain.

The reason is that, at least for a short period of time, the tension he is under has been relieved. He reports to himself that for these few precious moments he feels good again. No matter how much trouble there may be around him as a result of his drinking, he is still receiving positive reinforcement.

In alcoholism, the pain will always be intense in others before the alcoholic will feel pain. The spouse receives pain in the moderate stage, but the alcoholic is not going to stop drinking just because the spouse is hurting. When the physical or emotional pain becomes greater in him than in others around him, he will then reach his so-called "bottom."

The alcoholism field abounds with examples of the pain the alcoholic inflicts on others before he realizes there is a problem, or, if you will, before he feels pain.

A spouse of an alcoholic tried vainly to hide the family's blank checks from her alcoholic husband because he was writing them flagrantly without funds to cover them. She finally found a hiding place even he couldn't discover, but her husband found another way to continue his spending. This alcoholic had simply gone to the bank and asked for new checks, saying he had run out; the bank was happy to oblige. For her there was a great deal of emotional pain, yet for him the pain wasn't too great. He would not change his behavior of drinking and writing bad checks because of someone else's pain.

Another young alcoholic upon receiving much "static" from his wife over the amount of beer he was drinking decided to concede to her wishes. They agreed he would drink only three bottles of beer each evening. She could not emotionally tolerate more. That's when he started buying beer in quart bottles.

We human beings will not tolerate pain for any long period of time. Therefore, when we are operating under pain or tension, we must bring into play some form of behavior which will allow reduction of the tension. The alcoholic has a form of behavior that he has learned which operates for him very beautifully. He has found that if he takes into his system several martinis, for instance, the tension leaves and he can report a feeling of goodness within him.

Has he really done anything with this tension except cover it up temporarily? He has assumed a Band-Aid approach to a major problem. By covering up his problem with the sedative effects of alcohol, for a period of time there is *no* problem. It must be understood that the alcoholic is receiving positive reinforcement for his drinking behavior. Now suppose someone comes along and says, "Okay, Fred, give me the method you use to handle your tension; give it up, quit drinking!"

What's his logical answer? He'll probably say, "Get lost! You're not getting it from me. Why should I give up my way of handling pain?"

Obviously, this reaction is unconscious. Yet what the spouse or others are asking for, the alcoholic, literally, cannot give. If he gives it up, what happens to the tension? It's like taking the blanket away from the Peanuts character Linus—he comes "unglued." His tension will shoot straight up. He is thrust into a losing battle for security. Rather than risk this and to justify his behavior, the alcoholic will defend himself from any threatening situation. He does this in many ways. Generally speaking, he labels the spouse "dumb, stupid, and ignorant." Or he may say, "The job is no good, the boss doesn't understand me." "The minister is off his rocker." Once he can place the blame for his problems elsewhere, he is free to pursue his drinking.

Now that he has his justification, such as a spouse that doesn't understand him, he can continue his drinking. This deepens the pain of the spouse who continues her behavior of trying to get the alcoholic to stop drinking, and a vicious circle is easily recognizable. Accusations such as "If you loved me and if you loved the children you would stop drinking" only lead to increased drinking. If the alcoholic drinks to relieve tension, then such statements can only lead to increased drinking because it increases the tension. In fact, most of the "home remedies" used by nonalcoholics to stop the drinking of the alcoholic lead to increased drinking.

How do we get rid of tension? That's a tall order, and for my part, I feel that all of us will operate under some form of tension most of our lives. If the individual isn't concerned about his drinking, then it's the Russians dropping atomic bombs on his head. If it isn't Russians, then it's the high cost of living. If it isn't the high cost of living, then it's politics and on and on and on. In fact, some people will worry about not having anything to worry about if they can't find anything else!

Our procedure for treating the alcoholic must be directed toward treating the behavior. We want to find a substitute form to replace the drinking which will allow constructive reduction of tension. We are concerned only with changing the way the person reacts to tension. An unacceptable form of behavior is taken away and replaced with one which is acceptable. If this new behavior becomes a reward process for him, he will receive the necessary feelings of goodness from the substitute behavior. Involvement with A.A., avocations, and God produce substitute behavior more acceptable than the drinking behavior.

Behavior is learned; it is a product of hereditary and environmental processes. Therefore we can unlearn inappropriate behavior and learn new, acceptable forms of behavior.

Sounds simple, doesn't it? And in some ways, it is. The total person is a complex person, however, and we can't control all avenues of behavior through appropriate reinforcements. Another factor is that much of behavior is unconsciously motivated, which literally means that the person involved in a problem is not going to recognize that a problem exists. We may know by our feelings, our attitudes that something is wrong. We become motivated to handle the wrongs (conflicts in our lives) when the pain becomes greater than the feelings of goodness.

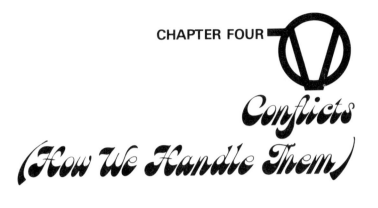

CHAPTER FOUR

Conflicts
(How We Handle Them)

Conflicts are a part of all of our lives and whether we show others adaptive or maladaptive behavior depends on how we handle the little and big conflicts in our lives.

A conflict occurs when we have two opposing systems operating and the two systems are of equal value: "Hmmm...should I have this piece of chocolate pie or should I choose that piece of chocolate cake?" Both things equal, we're in a conflict situation between two positive goals. Indecisiveness is always present in a conflict, and frankly, I feel that indecisiveness is a hallmark in alcoholism conflicts. Conflicts come in different varieties. They can be conscious—that is, we can know we're caught up in them—or they can be unconscious, i.e. having inferiority feelings and defending against them without knowledge. Conflicts, according to Kurt Lewin, come in one of three sizes but in varying degrees of severity:

1. A conflict between two positive goals (the cake and pie example).
2. A conflict between two negative goals (should I go for treatment or lose my wife).

3. A conflict between a positive goal and a negative goal (wanting a date with a beautiful girl and inferiority).

Each of these will be explained.

If I were to offer you a $500 bill in one hand and a $5 bill in the other, the choice would not be difficult. You would quickly choose the hand with the $500. What would happen, however, if I replaced the $500 with a $5 bill so both of my hands would have an equal amount? Would you be in a conflict? The answer, of course, is yes. For a brief moment in time, indecisiveness would be present; then, rather quickly you would make a choice. Reason: the receiving of the money would be for most a positive reward.

Perhaps one of the best ways of seeing this type of conflict in operation is to give a dime to a three- or four-year-old child, place him in front of a candy counter, and watch the choice process begin. Several minutes later the waiting mother shouts, "Make a choice or you don't get any candy." Once the equality is broken by the mother's voice, a choice is rapidly forthcoming, for after all, a candy bar of any kind is better than no candy bar at all. Let me diagram this for you:

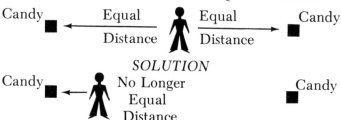

TWO POSITIVE GOALS OF EQUAL VALUE

Break up the equality and the decision becomes easy.

To further understand this problem, place yourself an equal distance from two things that you really want. Perhaps for you gals this could be a decision about buying a beautiful new dress or buying a stunning pants suit, or for you fellows, a choice between buying an Olds and a Buick of the same price range. You are caught in the middle equal distance from each goal. How do you resolve it? This one is easy. Perhaps your girl friend likes one dress better than the other or the sales clerk is good at her job. Either or both can influence your decision and break up the equality of your choices. Perhaps a good friend owns an Olds, or the Olds salesman is convincing, and you end up selecting the Olds. Both the new dress and the new car, regardless of choice, now have positive value to you and you report happiness to yourself. Easy to resolve? Yes, as long as you or someone else breaks the equality between the two equal value objects.

The next conflict is a choice between two negative goals. No matter which way you go, you will be punished. This problem is considerably more difficult to resolve because now there is punishment involved whichever way you move. Let's imagine this situation: On each side of you is a 260-pound Kansas City Chiefs' defensive tackle. These tackles have orders to rear back and hit you as hard as they can the moment you get close to them. Think of this in terms of your own feelings. We're going to have you approach the tackle on the left. What do you feel? Anxiety and worry are certainly present, and your tension level goes up. Tension is pain, and, as stated earlier, human beings will not tolerate pain if it can be avoided.

TWO NEGATIVE GOALS OF EQUAL VALUE

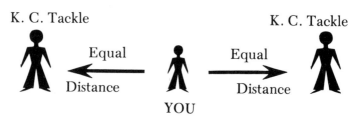

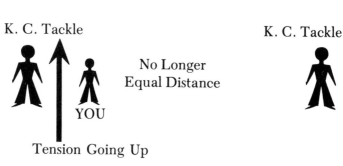

Which tackle looks safest?

As you are walking slowly toward the tackle on your left, he begins to assume negative value. After all, you don't really want to get hit. You look back at the tackle that you are going away from, and frankly, he doesn't look as bad as the one you're approaching. Why? The distance factor involved here is responsible. Your reaction? You turn around and start moving in the direction of the tackle that was on your right. Now as you get closer to him, the whole tension is experienced again and you are caught up in a vicious circle. What do you do? You can't go through life walking back and forth between these two men, so you look for other solutions. You do what in psychology is called "leaving the field." In a sense, you start looking for other ways of behaving that will allow you to avoid the conflict.

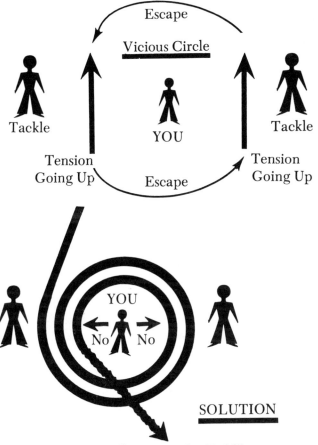

"Leaving the Field"

Round and round you go; where you end up I do know—you end up in the middle formulating a method of escape.

In alcoholism, this is sometimes referred to as a "geographic relocation." "Come on, dear, let's move to another town. They don't understand us here. I'll get a good job and we will start over." So you move—only one day you look up and there is one of those Kansas City Chiefs' tackles just waiting to hit you. So you get on the bus and run again. Actually, you can't run from a psychological problem; for the most part the problem is *you*, but this piece of knowledge isn't going to stop you from trying.

The alcoholic builds up a beautiful alibi system to handle this negative conflict. "I promise you I won't drink again." The water wagon approach to the problem is often the alcoholic's answer. What he means is he won't drink again until the pressure is off. "I can stop any time I want to. I don't need booze." What he's saying is that now that he's in trouble as a result of his drinking, he can stop until the problem hides its head.

No one really wants to be placed in a painful situation, and the "normal" way of handling it is to try to escape from it. From a psychological point of view, the escape comes from choosing other forms of behavior as illustrated.

If the pain of a problem is so great that a person must run from it, how can he face the pain? Some of the techniques used by spouses in vain attempts to force this confrontation are pouring the alcoholic's booze down the drain, hiding it from him so he can't drink so much, trying to offer him coffee at the right moment so that he won't choose liquor, curtailing his spending money, making countless threats, and finally coming through with the old standby, "If you loved me and the children you would stop drinking."

Would that recovery from alcoholism were so simple! Remember, the alcoholic is using alcohol to adjust "normally" and we come along and say, "Give us your normal behavioral adjustment pattern." Without a good substitute what would you answer? Take some object that is especially important to you. Then let me say, "Give it to me. You can never again use it." What would your answer be? I'm confident it would be, "No, you cannot have it," followed by whatever excuses or reasons you would have for not giving it up. The alcoholic will react the same way. He doesn't want to give up what's working for him, so the excuses start.

If in this stage of alcoholism you wait for the alcoholic to make the appropriate choice, his choice will be continued drinking. However, there is something you can do—and now I'm talking to those of you who love or hate the alcoholic—you can create a crisis in his life. This takes guts plus being in a position where you can apply pressure to force the alcoholic to face his problem. Yes, I mean force. I have never had an alcoholic run up the Valley Hope driveway with arms outstretched saying "Hallelujah, brother! Let me in for treatment." Most arrive with someone kicking them all the way. This may be a spouse who "promises" divorce, a judge who gave the alcoholic a choice between jail or treatment, or a boss who says get help or get out. This person can be anyone who cares enough to use "tough love" to get the alcoholic to look at himself. It is these people who love the alcoholic and/or hate his behavior that will finally force the alcoholic to face his problem. It means creating more pain in him than the pain he is avoiding.

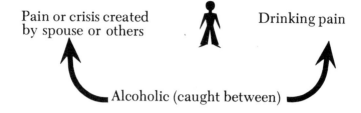

Pain or crisis created by spouse or others — Drinking pain — Alcoholic (caught between)

Let's return to the original problem posed in this chapter. Let's create a crisis in your life. We are going to introduce you to two offensive tackles of the Kansas City Chiefs. You are told that if you don't go over to get hit by the two defensive tackles you have already met, these two offensive tackles will bodily haul you over. You will scream, "You can't do this to me." You'll sputter, you'll make threats, you'll tell me what you'll do to me if I treat you like this. You'll use all your cunning and wiles to avoid the crisis, but because I love you, I'll order the tackles to pick you up, haul you over to your problem, and make you face it.

Defensive Tackle — Offensive Tackle — YOU — Offensive Tackle — Defensive Tackle

The two offensive tackles grab you by the arm and literally haul you over to get hit.

All the way over, you are fighting to avoid confrontation but to no avail. The superior strength of the tackles has brought you face-to-face with your problem. The defensive tackle rears back, and "Pow"—your problem has been faced. Your first feeling upon awakening, surprisingly, is one of relief; the second, anger and its expression.

This is the same situation as that faced by the spouse of the alcoholic committing him for treatment, or using separation or divorce to force him to get help. He, like you, will fight all the way, and it takes a great deal of "tough love" to force a loved one to help himself when he doesn't want the help.

From a psychological point of view, creating a crisis means to bring into play some factor which will create greater pain than the adjustment the alcoholic is using. He receives positive effects from his alcohol and he doesn't want to give it up. Somewhere along the line a form of behavior must be used that kicks the props out from under him and forces him to make the choice of accepting treatment. A judge does this beautifully when he states, "Thirty days in treatment or ninety days in jail." A boss also has a weapon at his command—treatment or no job.

In the positive-negative type of conflict, one is given a choice between a positive and a negative goal, a reward and punishment. Logically, it seems that anyone facing this choice would take the positive goal; however, the unconscious part of the conflict causes a problem within the person.

I would like to introduce you to Fred who has a feeling which leaves him with inner distress. He feels he is "less than" others. He has a feeling of inferiority.

This character defect is psychologically painful to Fred. Because it is, he will want to escape the pain. Fred could choose many ways of adjusting to his feelings of inferiority. He could become a fighter, a bully who knocks people around, all the while saying to himself, "I'm stronger than you are." Every time he beats someone, he feels that much better.

He could react by being a person with a "high need for social approval" (HNSA). Fred could go out of his way for a pat on the back. Since he cannot find his ego gratification within himself, he will do things for others who, in turn, will take care of his ego by telling him how wonderful he is.

He could also handle this feeling of inferiority through withdrawal. Nearly every person who is introverted is a person with some inferiority feelings. Withdrawal can take many forms. One can become an avid reader, a sleeper, a loner, or anything that will remove him from the source of the injury.

For sake of example, withdrawal will be the method we'll give Fred for handling his inferiority. He is a "shy guy," quiet, well liked, respected; he makes good grades, and doesn't appear to have many problems. But no one really knows Fred, including his teachers who have him sit in the back row because he is so "trustworthy."

Suppose Fred is a senior in high school and seventeen years old. One day, a beautiful girl by the name of Mary moves into the community. Fred takes one look at Mary and Cupid's arrow fells him. He is in love and wants to date Mary. Seems simple, doesn't it? Just pick up a phone, call her, and ask for the date. But—what if Mary says, "No"?

The date is Fred's positive goal while the possibility of rejection from Mary is the negative goal.

DATE   👤   ——   REJECTION

FRED

What complicates the situation is that unknown to Fred, inferiority is rearing its head. Even though it is unconscious, it can and does dominate his behavior. Fred is unsure of himself. This is psychologically painful, and he will work very hard not to place himself in a position of psychological pain. What happens is that Fred becomes what I refer to as an "If maybe" person. "If I call Mary maybe she will go out with me" is better in terms of ego than calling Mary and being turned down. Any rejection would heighten the feeling of inferiority which creates pain. It is this pain that Fred tries to avoid by instituting his defenses.

The more Fred sees Mary, the more he knows he has to go out with her. One day as he's walking down the street he notices a phone. Now is the time. He confidently walks inside, picks up the phone, and proceeds to dial. With each digit he gets a funny feeling somewhat like fear. Psychological pain is on its way, and the quickest way for him to relieve this is to quit dialing. We now have a six-digit dialer on our hands! Fred walks away from the booth and begins to experience some relief from the tension. The farther away he gets the more the tension is relieved and he begins talking to himself and saying, "You fool." He may chastise himself to the point of going back to the booth to try again, but as he heads back the tension begins to increase again.

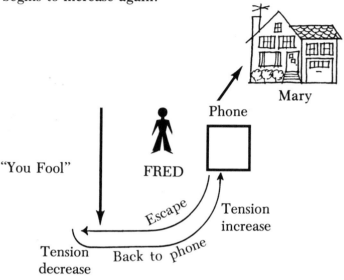

Poor Fred can't keep going through this situation all his life, so we'll have Fred's best friend Joe enter the scene. Joe sees Fred going to the phone booth and says, "Hey, Fred, what are you doing?" Without thinking, Fred says he's going to call Mary for a date. Now he has another positive-negative conflict. He wants Joe to like him, but if he doesn't call Mary he will be a "chicken" in Joe's eyes. The problem with Joe is that he is closer, so in a sense, Fred has had it. He walks into the booth, dials seven digits, and the phone rings at Mary's house.

Since we are making up this story, let's consider two possible situations. Suppose Mary says, "Heavens, no. What makes you think I'd ever go out with you?" When Fred comes out of the booth, he isn't showing his hurt, rather he is rationalizing his failure by mumbling, "What makes her think she's the only girl in the world? Who would want to go out with her anyway?" Joe, however, has witnessed Fred's failure. In the future, whenever Fred sees Joe he will be reminded of his failure and possibly will avoid Joe. This friendship could break down because while Fred is avoiding Joe, Joe doesn't know what's happening. He, more than likely, is thinking that Fred has become a snob. Fred may lose Joe as well as Mary and feel even more inferior.

Then let's assume that Mary is delighted when Fred calls her and gladly accepts his invitation for a date. Now as Fred comes bouncing out of the phone booth, the friendship between Joe and him will blossom—Joe has witnessed success. Now that the ice is broken, phone calls will be frequent, and the odds are that Fred will want to go "steady." Why? Who in their "right" mind would want to go through the agony of asking another girl for a date again?

Everything has been going well with Fred and Mary as the time for the senior prom approaches. Fred asks Mary and Joe asks Joann for dates to the dance and are accepted. They are now sitting at their table having great fun when Joe does a "stupid thing," stupid in terms of Fred's inferiority: he asks Joann to dance. Now this puts Fred into another conflict. He feels he should ask Mary to dance, too. He knows if he does ask her, he may look like a fool on the dance floor because he doesn't really know how to dance.

Enter the villain called Slim. He says, "Fred, come out to the car; I've got something for you." At this point Fred would go with anybody just to avoid the situation. Lo and behold, Slim has a jug in his car and offers Fred a drink. Fred doesn't get drunk, but an amazing things happens after the ingestion of a couple of drinks: he can rejoin Mary and ask her to dance.

The alcohol which is a sedative chemical has become a positive reinforcement. It has allowed the sedation of Fred's inhibition, judgment, and reasoning and has given him a feeling of exhilaration. He can do now what he normally would not do.

As Fred dances with Mary, he is further reinforced by her behavior. All she has to do is smile and he is rewarded. Joe looks over and says, "Wow, I don't believe it. I've never seen you on the dance floor before, Fred. You're pretty good." And Joann "nails the lid on the coffin" by saying, "You save me a dance, Fred." All these are operating as positive secondary reinforcements.

Now, when Fred goes to his next dance, will he trust Slim to bring the jug or will Fred bring it? Alcoholics going through Valley Hope with problems similar to Fred's state categorically that they "sure wouldn't trust old Slim to bring the bottle." They would have their own.

Learning has taken place. With the ingestion of the alcohol, Fred has become a dancer. Not only does he become a dancer but more importantly he becomes accepted. The truth of the matter is that he has found a Fred he likes and, I suspect, a Fred that he is going to try to keep. For a period of time it seems his inferiority doesn't exist. The chemical alcohol becomes a medical Band-Aid that covers his imperfections. Under its influence Fred is better liked by himself and others. He has discovered a new way of behavior; he has learned that if he takes three, four, or five drinks he becomes "normal."

INFERIORITY + ALCOHOL = REDUCED FEELINGS OF INFERIORITY
(Psychological Pain)

As we go through life with Fred, any time he finds himself in a situation in which he must make a choice, he will experience feelings of tension or pain. Suppose, for example, that Fred must choose between two jobs: for a period of time he will feel psychological pain. However, he has learned that if he takes a few drinks, the choice will be simpler. (By the way, this learning is unconscious—i.e. without awareness by Fred.)

A couple of drinks will ease the tension, and choices become easier—at least they seem so to Fred, and it's what Fred thinks that's important to Fred.

As life progresses it also becomes more complicated; more and more conflict choice situations are inevitable. Let's suppose that Fred and Mary get married. Does this lessen adjustments for Fred? Certainly not; now he has many varieties of adjustments to make such as, Do we rent or do we buy? Should we get a sports car or a station wagon? Sexual adjustments are part of the picture. All sorts of questions will arise, but the major problem is the necessity for two unique human beings to adjust to each other.

The marriage goes along fairly well until a child enters the family unit. The blessings of a child are also compounding the problem of inferiority. Mary's time is now split and she cannot devote full time to Fred. That old feeling of rejection returns. There is a way to handle it: a couple of drinks with the boys or a few to relax.

So we have a young man with a problem, but also the young man has a solution to the problem. His solution is found in the sedative effects of a chemical called alcohol. As long as this type of behavior works positively for Fred, he will continue to use it. However, in the lives of people using alcohol as a solution to a problem, there will come a day when someone will say just as Mary says to Fred, "Fred, you're drinking too much." Now Fred is thrown into a perpetual state of conflict. Why? Fred loves Mary— she disapproves of his drinking—Fred needs drinking for stability.

This is when the individual begins to move into the acquired state of alcoholism. The beginning of the alibi system may originate at this point: Lying, cheating, and hiding of the bottle as well as many other types of avoidance behavior will occur.

Mary must become the scapegoat. Fred must have anger from her to justify drinking. From here on, we find the rapid deterioration of the family, and Fred is thrown into the vicious downward spiral of alcoholism. Fred loves Mary regardless of what he says or does to the contrary. Most alcoholics are very sensitive people, not insensitive clods as is often thought.

Now we are beginning to move back to a conflict situation because the pain has become so great for Mary that she eventually will bring about a crisis. Mary will say, "Fred, I've had it. You must do something about your drinking." And old Fred is going to come up fighting, scratching, kicking, and screaming. Sooner or later, someone like Mary who has been caused a great deal of pain by the alcoholic's drinking will put a stop to the vicious circle. And Fred is faced with two negative type behaviors. During the preceding years of this progressive illness, Fred has learned to defend himself, and like most alcoholics, he has learned his lessons well. In fact, he has learned his lesson so well that without the help of others his defenses will allow him to continue drinking.

CHAPTER FIVE

What Protects Me (Defenses)

An alcoholic walked into my office some time back, sat down, indicated he wanted to enter Valley Hope for treatment, and proceeded to tell me how much money he was making. He stated that he was a "supersalesman" for a soft water dealer and any time he went out to sell he made a "big deal." According to him, he averaged $2,000 a month, had a beautiful house, two cars, three televisions, and so on. I listened intently but I felt that I was once again dealing with a "phony," a person we call the "Big I." I asked him for a down payment and he gave detailed reasons why he could not pay. Now I knew I had a phony. His reasons were phony to me, but they were not phony to him. He needed that "Big I" approach to life. It was really the only thing on which he could pin his self-respect. He wasn't comfortable with it, but he needed it. He had to convince others that he was something more than nothing. He had to have a defense to protect and to enhance himself even if it were nothing more than to do this in his own eyes.

Human behavior, in my estimation, is designed to protect us from the external and internal stress generated by our day-to-day living. Defense mechanisms are quite simply forms of behavior designed to make us feel comfortable. They are natural and are needed by all of us. As I tell about several mechanisms I see most frequently in addiction processes, you will find they are defenses you use too. Keep in mind that all our defenses are designed to protect us and all of us need protection. Defenses make for difficulties only when they control us rather than our controlling them.

Anytime we are under tension, whether that tension is pleasurable or painful, there will be a behavioral action to that tension. Why? Well, we want to experience more of a good thing and less of a bad. Since we are talking about alcoholism and related addictions, we will concentrate on negative tension, the kind that causes us pain. No one wants to be hurt. We would all rather feel comfortable. What do we do when we get a headache? The usual behavior is to get an aspirin or two and wait for the pain to disappear. In a sense, this is what we do with our defenses; we feel pain, we go to the medicine cabinet (our mind), and call for our favorite aspirin (defense mechanism). If it works we will store it away for use again and again when similar conditions arise.

The major defense used by the alcoholic and the one which causes him the greatest difficulty is a defense called *denial*. Denial, the ability to ignore a problem, is not an uncommon defense. A lump in the breast is "ignored" until it is too large to ignore. "I can't have a social disease; I haven't done anything wrong" is yet another form of denial. We could go on and on, but let's look at how the alcoholic uses denial.

An alcoholic was drinking so much, so fast, and showing such severe declension in his personal habits that his spouse restricted him to the basement of his home while he was drinking. He would at times defecate, urinate, and vomit on himself during his drinking bouts. His spouse, the martyred soul that she was, would clean him up and put him to bed. He would awaken the next day in a blackout with no apparent knowledge of his behavior. The spouse, finally unable to tolerate any more, called us for help. We suggested that she use "tough love" and allow the alcoholic the privilege of facing his own reality. The objections came hot and heavy from the spouse. She couldn't be that mean; she loved him and he needed her. These were all defenses to protect herself from the stigma of her husband's alcoholic behavior.

We went over to the house, into the basement, and there found him lying in all his shining—or shall we say, stinking—glory. We didn't want him to escape the privilege of his own reality, so we rigged a large mirror which would enable him to view himself first thing upon awakening. This alcoholic awoke, raised himself up, looked in the mirror, and denied—yes, denied—that the reflection in the mirror was indeed his own image.

The sequel: two days later this alcoholic entered treatment. I wish I could report that the treatment was effective and that he came to grips with his problem, but he didn't. I have always wondered if his spouse ever tried the mirror again.

In alcohol addiction this story is more common than uncommon, and the inability of the alcoholic to see his alcoholism is acted out in many different ways and for long periods of time.

We ask two questions routinely of alcoholics going through Valley Hope. Have you ever been told by anyone that you drink "too much"? If so, when if ever did you seek help for the problem of "too much"? The time between confrontation (too much) and the first help sought is unhappily an average of 13.5 years, as we discussed in an earlier chapter. We ask the alcoholic to take a good look at denial. Usually he will not recognize this defense, and someone who cares about him will have to create pressure to "force" him to recognize his problem. This means that someone is going to have to create a crisis in the life of the alcoholic; commitment, separation, divorce are methods of "tough love" often needed to break the defense. Denial by itself will weaken as the disease progresses, but it seems a tragedy for the alcoholic to hit "bottom" or his own destruction when the "bottom" can be raised through the efforts of someone who cares.

"Tough love" is just what it says—tough. It is not easy to say to a loved one, "I love you and cannot stand by and watch you slowly drink yourself to death." It is not easy to punish a small child for playing with something which is dangerous or may harm him; it creates pain in you and in the child. But because you love that child, you use "tough love" and force him to stop whatever it is that may cause him harm. This is the same thing that family members are forced to do for alcoholics: they must make the pain great enough for the alcoholic that the pain of ceasing to drink becomes the "lesser of two evils."

Projection is another defense utilized by the

alcoholic. It involves placing blame on others for our own unacceptable acts. This is such a beautiful defense and it works so well for the alcoholic that generally the "spouse of the souse" ends up on the psychiatrist's couch before the alcoholic sees a need for help. This defense allows the individual to project blame for problems elsewhere, usually on to a loved one such as a spouse. She is told for so many years by the alcoholic that she is stupid and incompetent that she begins to believe it herself. This projection of blame may also be directed toward the job, friends, or town, but whatever direction it takes, the idea is always present that the alcoholic is a victim of circumstances. His problems are due to those around him or to circumstances, but never to any of his own doings.

A female spouse entered treatment at Valley Hope with her husband. Her tested I.Q. was 137 which she refused to believe. It had to be wrong because she just knew she was "dumb." At least this is what she had been told for many years by her alcoholic spouse. She really felt to blame for his drinking. Nice way out for the alcoholic, isn't it? It's quite common for the spouse of the alcoholic to get help for the problem before the alcoholic does. Projection, used properly, can be an excellent defense for the person using it because he is never to blame for the problems which exist. For the person projection is used on, it is a very painful defense. One can only be "blamed" so much for problems before there is a tendency to believe that he or she is responsible. Then there is a need to be removed from the stress situation.

The following story is a frequently occurring illustration of how this defense works. An alcoholic friend of mine would come home in the evening to find a clean, spotless house. Upon finding the house this way, he would become violently angry at his wife and yell, "My God, woman, you keep this house so clean no one can live in it. You're driving me crazy." With that he would slam the door as he made his grant exit to go out and drink. The next night he would come home to a "messy" house, but he would explode again, "My God, woman, this house is so dirty I can't live in it. You're driving me out of my mind." It isn't any wonder the spouse sought help before the alcoholic!

If you think you are the "spouse of a souse" then try to understand that what the drinker is doing is projecting his own image of self-hatred onto you. Then if he can succeed in getting you angry, the image is verified; and from his point of view, you (the spouse) are now at fault, thus allowing him to do as he pleases. The Al-Anon slogan of "Let Go and Let God" can be of primary importance in a recovery program for the spouse of an alcoholic and for the alcoholic as well. Al-Anon is a self-help group, a fellowship of men and women, old and young alike, who are relatives and/or friends of alcoholics. In Al-Anon those people who are closest to the alcoholic and who are affected most by his drinking bind together to share their experience, strength, and hope. It is a beautiful program like Alcoholics Anonymous and for many has become a way of life in which they can find growth regardless of whether they are living with a practicing or sober alcoholic. This type of self-help program can weaken the defense of projection used by the alcoholic through understanding what the alcoholic is trying to do.

Rationalization is the defense of making logical excuses. The key word in this defense is "logical." It has got to make sense to the person using it but not necessarily to anyone else. This defense is best illustrated by the terrible disease that strikes the average American called "new caritis." This is the disease that new car salesmen love because it means they will make a sale.

The rationalization goes like this. First look at what you will have to do to the "old buggy" if you decide to trade cars. The tires are bad, and you'll need new ones if you keep it instead of trading. The battery is three years old and the guarantee has run out. The upholstery is torn and dirty, the paint is bad and somewhat faded. The crowning blow comes as you are driving down the street and you hear a strange noise in the engine—now you know you have to trade. Miraculously, once you have decided to trade and particularly as you dicker with the salesman, the old buggy becomes "old reliable" again.

I've had personal experience with this defense. I had always wanted to get a "bigger car." I took a job in North Dakota where it is common knowledge that there are long distances between towns. I rationalized that if I had a bigger car I would arrive at my destination more relaxed and would be able to do more and better work. Oh, yes, I forgot to mention that I also had back surgery and a scar was left on my back which caused me some minor pain, thus making a bigger car a necessity for my comfort.

Rationalization is not always recognizable but it is one of the easier defenses to see. It is used many, many times a day by everyone to insure peace and tranquillity.

One alcoholic discussed how he used rationalization to further his drinking habits. "During my drinking days I left work about 4:15 p.m. nearly every day of the week. I decided that I would miss the heavy traffic if I stayed at the bar for an hour or so. Back I would go to the bar. I avoided the heavy traffic all right. It was usually 12:30 or 2:00 a.m. before I made it home (if I did at all)."

Another alcoholic said he used to love going to parties so much that he rationalized that he really should be ready for the party when the time came, so he would start drinking about 10:00 a.m. the day of the party. When he arrived home from work after drinking all day he would find his wife so upset with him that she would refuse to go to the party. Drowning his sorrows, he would drink more and often pass out and miss the party entirely.

A friend of mine indicated that he really hated to go to parties, for at most parties only two or three drinks were served. In his opinion it was hardly worth the effort to go. He handled his difficulty quite nicely, however, by volunteering to become the bartender, for, as he stated, he was "always willing to help other people."

Another alcoholic acquaintance indicated he had to carry a flask with him at all times because he was never sure when a friend would ask for a drink, and if he didn't have a drink to offer he would feel very uncomfortable.

Some justify the expense of their drinking by the fact that their wives spend a considerable amount of money for clothing.

The examples of this type of defense are really numerous. If you do become familiar with the logical excuses of the rationalization process you'll be able to see them in operation many times during the course of any given day. It is much easier to see these in operation in others than in ourselves, however.

Aggression is another form of defense. People with strong inferiority feelings will often use this method.

An alcoholic friend still in the practicing stage of his illness used to go into a bar, line up the male customers, look them straight in the eye, and calmly inform them that the first one who moved would be "pulverized." The first one who moved was hit and the fight was on. Soon the police were on their way. If three policemen were sent, our alcoholic friend would go in peace, chest pushed out, and proud of the fact that three policemen had to be sent for him. If only one policeman showed up, however, the fight continued.

It seemed to one aggressive alcoholic that he was always getting into so much trouble with his drinking that all he had to do was go glug-glug-glug, sit down and wait, and within thirty minutes the police were there.

I believe that the feelings defended by aggression are many times those of inferiority, the feeling of being "less than." In the mind of the aggressor to outfight someone indicates superiority over that person. Verbal aggression is also part of this defense, and the verbal attack like the physical one is designed to make one more than, not less than, someone else. In many ways, aggression simply pushes people away and is really indicating the attitude, "If I don't let anyone close to me then no one can hurt me." Many alcoholics are fighters but an even greater percentage of them handle their problems with the defense of withdrawal.

Withdrawal is removing oneself from the source of the injury or from the source of pain, and thus it protects. As an example, a friend became involved in an affair. The use of the beverage alcohol was also involved. This man at the outset of this situation was a religious individual, not a religious "nut," but he had a comfortable relationship with his God as he understood Him. He was married and had two children. The marriage would have been termed "rocky."

This man's conscience operated very well and as the affair continued the feelings of guilt became overwhelming. To counter the guilt he employed the defense of withdrawal. First he became very angry with the community in which he was living, indicating that no one could get anywhere with the type of people in that town. Obviously, there was also some projection involved in this, but what he was saying was, "In order to feel comfortable I have to remove myself from anyone who could accuse me of infidelity." His second move was to begin to withdraw from community and civic affairs. He dropped his membership in several service clubs, again with the idea of protecting himself from having to face these people should they ever find out. His next move was to pull away from his Higher Power, and he dropped out of church as a result. The next step in his withdrawal was in relationship to his job. He tried to become a self-employed person, but when this did not work to his satisfaction he moved to another town. All of these activities took place over a period of slightly more than a year.

As each withdrawal step took place the drinking increased until finally he had to seek help. A recovery program based on insight into the method of defense he was using has now been established.

The introverted type of personality (and in the field of alcoholism there are many that refer to this) is one that bottles his feelings up inside himself and doesn't express these to significant others in his life. Usually this type of person uses withdrawal as a form of defense, retreating further and further into himself and removing himself from the closeness of loved ones. He actually has only one sounding board for the realities of life. Unfortunately, this sounding board has to be himself, and since he is the one instituting withdrawal as a basic defense, he can only continue to utilize it. Many times the reality of withdrawal is driven home very sharply when others are hurt. Then the individual is forced to look at himself. As human beings we do not tolerate pain. When pain is forced on us we attempt to recognize and eliminate the source of the pain.

Another form of defense is that known as a *conversion reaction*. This means that we convert emotional problems into physical ones. Perhaps this is because physical illness is more acceptable to many than emotional illness. One of Valley Hope's physicians reported reading in a medical journal that 60 percent of the patients seen by medical doctors have emotional problems manifesting themselves in physical difficulties.

Recently we had a spouse in treatment who hadn't spoken a word in nine years. Medical tests were negative. It was concluded that she had an emotional disability. Once the marital and alcohol problems were handled in her family, her voice returned, and she was able to talk. She began doing public speaking and was a guest speaker at a state A.A. conference.

Headaches are considered by many to be emotionally induced. It is difficult to see physical problems as a defense form since the pain is actually present. The headaches are there and they hurt. Most people cannot believe that physical pain can be mentally produced, but time and time again alcoholics as well as their spouses present a picture of physical problems with no physical basis.

Conversion is probably one of the most common defenses and can be seen in many different forms. They vary from severe ones such as hysterical blindness and deafness to simple annoying headaches.

One individual I had in treatment had an overpowering urge to kill his wife. He could not tolerate the amount of anxiety engendered by this thought. His right arm became paralyzed from the elbow to the wrist and hand. Upon having a neurological examination, no reason for the paralysis was found. Through consultation we found that he had these intense feelings about his wife. Although the marriage ended in a divorce, at least partial success was achieved. Once the divorce was granted, he regained normal use of his arm.

Perhaps one of the more common conversion reactions is the "tiredness" syndrome in which an individual simply doesn't have the energy to do the things he knows he has to do. This is the type of person who comes home from work, goes to the couch, picks up the paper, and immediately falls asleep. In one sense, it is a form of withdrawal, but the conversion of emotional problems to a physical tiredness is also present.

There are many who consider a conversion reaction an illness in and of itself. I see it as a reaction to stress situations the individual is placed in and therefore a defense against undue stress.

Displacement is the discharging of pent-up feelings inside us. Usually these feelings are causing a great deal of anger and hostility, and we place this anger and hostility on objects that are considerably less dangerous to us than those which have aroused these feelings within us.

An alcoholic on a recovery program handled his anger by working in his workshop. The amount of woodwork he produced was an indication of the type of month he had had, a great deal meant he had had a very bad month emotionally. This would be an example of *appropriate displacement.* Some clean the house from top to bottom, stem to stern, when they become angry. Others may throw a pot or pan or slam doors. All of these are examples of displacement.

A psychologist has expressed the theory that a great number of highway accidents are caused by displacement. This is not an unreal assumption. I ask people if they have ever floorboarded a car when they were angry; a "yes" answer is quite common. It is obvious that if one's mind is focused in anger on an event his full attention cannot be given to driving a car, and the chances of accidents are greatly increased. Displacement is a rather childish defense; it actually takes regression through anger, and regression invariably indicates immaturity.

Introjection is a little more difficult to understand as a defense. What takes place is that the alcoholic internalizes whatever the threatening situation is. He feels if it is internalized at least he has control of the situation and that it can now be handled.

The alcoholic begins to internalize the external values of society and in so doing has to become very subjective in his evaluation of himself. As the alcoholism continues, the individual begins to have a consistently bad image of himself. When he comes into treatment, we literally can say as many bad things about him as we desire and he will be nodding and congratulating us on our astute observations. However, if we turn the tables on him and indicate that there are very many positive attributes about him that should be recognized, he is not quite so willing to go along. As he sees it society indicates that alcoholism is bad; therefore, with the introjection of the external value systems of society he must also recognize that he is bad.

There are of course many other defenses, but I would like to end with *identification* because this defense is utilized very often by the alcoholic. Feelings of worth are increased by identifying with things that are happening around one.

Probably the simplest way to experience this defense is to go to a movie in which the heroine is having a great deal of trouble. Sympathy is aroused. People in the audience may be crying. What they are doing is identifying with the feelings of the star.

Many commercials are planned to take advantage of this process of identification. Situations are created which present drinking as being one of the activities of a real man. "He can hold his liquor like a man." "I can drink you under the table any time I want to."

Drinking often becomes synonymous with "I'm a man." This is quite evident with teen-age drinking.

Valley Hope has a cup-hanging ceremony which makes use of the principle of identification. After a patient has completed thirty days of treatment, a ceremony is held in which he hangs a cup on the wall. His spouse similarly hangs a saucer. It has become a custom among the patients to paint elaborate decorations and symbols on their cups and saucers. Often these relate to their feelings of sobriety and the new life they hope to embark on as they leave. It is usually a very emotional and meaningful ceremony. These cups and saucers are symbols of great significance to the patients. When a person resumes drinking, his cup is removed from the wall. This has a great impact on the other patients as well as on the patient who has had a relapse. When a former patient dies, a black ribbon is tied around his cup which acts as yet another symbol.

What we are attempting to do with the symbolism of the cup hanging is to tie it to sobriety. We are hoping that the alcoholic will "identify" his cup hanging in its place of honor at Valley Hope with sobriety.

Defenses as a general rule operate at an unconscious level. The fact that we don't realize we are utilizing helps enhances the defense. If we knew we were using denial, for example, it would be less effective. It is the unconscious element of the defenses that often makes it necessary to have another person show us our behavior. We are too close to it to be objective. It is also this unawareness that can allow a defense to control us. No rational man is going to allow a defense of denial to add 13.5 years of "hell" to his life if he has knowledge concerning this defense. It is the lack of knowledge of how we are protecting ourselves that allows the defense to control us rather than the reverse.

I believe very strongly that these defenses are designed to enhance an individual; even when the defenses get out of control they are still designed to protect and to make the individual feel better. However, it is when they get out of control that major problems in their utilization begin.

It is considered normal to utilize all of these defenses at one time or another. No doubt they were recognized as having been employed by each of us. We, as human beings, are not going to allow ourselves to be put into the position of jeopardizing our sense of personal worth. We are going to bring into play any type of adjustment mechanism we can which will allow us to enhance ourselves. I suspect all behavior is designed to enhance and to protect.

When one looks at the chronic alcoholic it is very difficult for a "rational" individual to say that that behavior is protecting the alcoholic. All that is seen is the terrible destruction the behavior is causing; however, when one looks at the alcoholic and at what he is attempting to do, it can quickly be recognized that his behavior is designed to enhance and protect himself.

CHAPTER SIX

Dynamics of Human Adjustment

In the last few chapters I've "splintered" things in the hope that they would be better understood. In this chapter we will take the splinters, glue them together, and try to make a whole. Hopefully when we are finished, we will be able to see that behavior operates as a whole, and the majority of the time our defenses are operating so well that we are unaware of why we do things; we just go ahead and do them. All of us have goals. Anytime we have a goal we are automatically a motivated organism. Any goal we have requires an expenditure of energy, some type of response which will allow us successfully to obtain the goal. Any goal attainment requires action on our part.

The best way to reach any goal is to get into action and head straight for the goal. Unfortunately, attainment of a goal is not quite that simple. Life is much too complicated.

For example, let's say it's Sunday morning and you decide you want to go to church. You're lying in bed when that decision is made. Immediately, there are innumerable barriers which have to be faced. Getting out of bed, dressing, eating, walking, driving—all are barriers to the achievement of your goal of attending church. Each one must be overcome if you are to attain the goal. All of life is like this; every time a goal is set there will be barriers in the way.

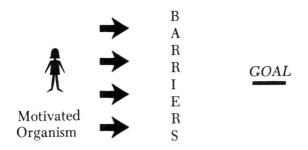

B
A
R
R
I
E
R
S

GOAL

Motivated
Organism

Every single person on the way to a goal bumps into a barrier. It may be nothing more than the energy required to reach the goal. Suppose you're sitting in a comfortable chair and you want to switch television channels to watch another program. It takes effort to get up and do this. That effort is a barrier. Whatever you're doing requires effort.

Whether you are going to be adjusted (normal) or maladjusted (abnormal) is not necessarily determined by your goal but by how you react to the barriers on your way to the goal.

Let's take a look at Fred and Mary. After several years of marriage Fred is sitting in his favorite chair in the living room and Mary is in the kitchen. Fred suddenly has an urge to go out for a drink. Drinking has already been causing problems between Fred and Mary, so somehow he has to get by that barrier in the kitchen called Mary. He thinks a few moments and then calls out, "Hey, Mary, part of my newspaper is missing and I'm going down to Jack's drugstore for a new one."

Mary's ears perk up, and she says to herself, "Ahuh, I've heard this one before—he wants to drink, and I'm not going to let him." So she replies to Fred, "That's wonderful, darling; give me a few minutes to finish the dishes and I'll go with you. I need to get out of the house." Now that's not exactly what Fred had in mind. His goal was a drink, not a walk to the corner drugstore.

Fred's first try to reach his goal (the drink) resulted in a miserable failure. He came up against the barrier on his way to his goal and he was "thrown for a loss." The result of failure to obtain the goal at this point is irritating and frustrating. Now to obtain his goal he has to regroup his forces. He falls back from the barrier and tries again. "I just remembered, dear, that I have to stop by Jerry's house. I had a business appointment with him, and we're supposed to talk over a big deal." Fred then sits back confidently waiting for Mary's answer.

She says, "Great, Fred, I haven't seen Janie [Jerry's wife] in several weeks; it will be nice to talk with her." Try No. 2 is a failure. Reaction: anger, more frustration, lower tolerance. Fred regroups again and hits the barrier for the third time.

"I can't wait for you to finish the dishes. Anyway this house is so ___ ___ ___ ___ dirty! Why don't you stay home and clean it up so a person wouldn't have to live in a pigpen?"

Fred needs an angry reply, and he has stated his position so the anger from his spouse is forthcoming. Mary replies, "It's your house, too; if you would take an interest in it and spend more time at home maybe it wouldn't be so messy."

Now Fred can attack in full force. "What do you mean I should spend more time at home? All of my time is spent making you a home. You're frightened that I'm going out to drink, and by God, I am!" The door slams and Fred is on his way to his goal completely justified, at least in his mind, for his behavior because he has that "stupid, ignorant, nagging wife at home who doesn't understand him."

Let's diagram what we have just said, hopefully to make it easier to understand the dynamics of the game these two people have been playing.

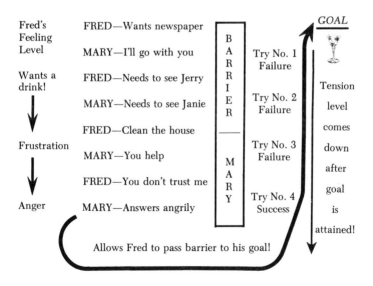

Let's look at the feeling level. Fred's first attempt fails. This results in frustration and a lower tolerance level. He regroups and makes his second effort. This, too, fails and results in more frustration and anger. Fred makes a third attempt by projecting blame to Mary (her poor housekeeping). Mary responds with anger, and Fred, also very angry, can leave the house knowing full well that all he wanted was a newspaper, saying to himself, "To heck with it. If she thinks I will drink, I'll show her." This entire episode of his drinking is justified in Fred's mind, for it was obviously Mary's fault. She does not understand him.

From Mary's point of view as Fred keeps repeating this behavior time after time, deep resentments set in and she begins to feel that he doesn't care for her—he would rather have booze than her. She wants to know why he keeps doing the same thing. Yet, we have to ask, too, why does she keep repeating her behavior? Both are concerned with their own feelings and wishes; each is hurt by the other. They have no time to try to understand each other since they are wrapped up in their own problems. They are busy playing the game that Paul Tournier speaks of as the "dialogue of the deaf."

If you were to ask Mary why she reacted the way she did, she would say very sincerely, with genuine concern and perhaps tears, that she was trying to keep Fred from drinking. Actually, by playing the game, she was helping remove the barrier to his goal of getting the drink. In many ways she actually aided him in the attainment of his goal.

If, at the beginning of this little game, she had said, "Fine, go get the newspaper," and added, "I hope you don't drink," she would have been letting go of him. She couldn't have stopped his behavior anyway. However, had she let go of him at the beginning instead of when the game was over, he could have justified his drinking, but the justification would have been very weak; he could have not rationalized it as well.

This is why we emphasize treatment of the spouse at our center; she must realize that she has problems also and can contribute to the husband's problems.

Let's go back to Fred. He butts his head against a barrier time after time and cannot circumvent it. If every time he does this he records a failure, then eventually a different type of behavior will emerge.

Assuming I am correct when I indicate that barriers are erected in all goal behavior, then reaction to the barrier in terms of success or failure will predict behavior. Successful goals lead to pleasant feelings and need not be discussed here. However, failure leads to pain. Because we will not tolerate pain for too long a period of time, when pain is encountered we will find some form of behavior that allows us the escape from that pain.

An alcoholic in treatment at Valley Hope had set a goal of trying to save $200,000 by the time he was forty. He felt very strongly about the need for the $200,000 and had outlined his program of action to attain the goal. He was thirty-one years old at the time his plan was put into effect. His plan: (1) he would keep his $8,500 a year job; (2) he would get a real estate license and sell property; (3) he would sell motivational tapes to make the rest of the money he needed. His plan denied reality. There was no way he could save $200,000 in nine years. When told that his plan was not feasible, he refused to accept this assessment. As the years passed, it became more and more apparent that the goal was unrealistic and the barriers to the goal were insurmountable. The amount of pain generated by the barriers became so great that sobriety "went out the window" and he returned to excessive drinking. He now indicates that if he hadn't started drinking again he would have achieved his goal, and through the use of the defense of projection his family and friends are the culprits in his failure; it is their fault that he returned to drinking, not his.

Basically what happened was that the barriers to his goal of saving $200,000 could not be circumvented. He would not change his goal so he had to do something about the pain encountered from not accomplishing the goal. He chose deviant behavior—a return to drinking—as an alternative to personal failure. He could blame his drinking on others, thus giving him an out. His choice of returning to drinking was simply to protect his self-esteem. He returned to drinking with full realization of the consequences of his behavior. The punishment from drinking was less than the punishment of failure. It gave him an "acceptable" way out of his dilemma.

In a sense this is similar to the behavior of a friend of mine who made a habit of going to the movies the night before a big college test. If he passed the test he was smart because he didn't have to study, but if he failed he blamed it on the fact that he had gone to the movies. He had a way out no matter what happened.

If a person cannot find a form of behavior that will allow partial success of goal attainment, then he is in for severe trouble. What happens with repeated failure is that an individual will build his own world. In other words, he leaves the world of reality. We then pin the classification of psychotic on him. No one is going to allow pain to dominate his life continually. If pain is consistent, some form of behavior will evolve to allow relief and that includes "flipping out."

More often than not the behavior selected runs contrary to what is considered by society as "normal." Then there is more trouble, for the chosen behavior is unacceptable to significant others in one's life. Because it inflicts pain on them, they want a change which again makes the life the goal seeker has chosen as being "normal" for him intolerable.

There are some criteria of what is "normal" behavior. Normal is that behavior which is acceptable to the society in which one lives. This allows a great deal of flexibility but there is a point at which people will become uneasy with "different" behavior, and the pressure will start.

This reminds me of a man who lived alone. He had the annoying habit of mowing his lawn backwards. He had a push-type mower which he would pull instead of push. His neighbors considered him an odd, peculiar guy anyway, and this was the "last straw." They petitioned this man's children to commit him to the state hospital. When he was evaluated, his diagnosis was simple schizophrenia. We didn't feel he would make a personality change, so we sent a person out to talk to his neighbors to try to get them to change their attitudes toward this man. If he is still living, I'll bet he is still mowing his lawn backwards. But it's okay now because his neighbors can accept what was once to them unacceptable behavior. He obviously is not seen as completely "normal" but because of the acceptance of him by others he can again resume his own adjustment.

What is normal? There are several traits which are generally considered "normal":

No. 1—A normal person can deny immediate gratification of his wishes. He can tolerate some pain and doesn't have to go off the deep end as a result of it. One of the major characteristics of alcoholic patients is lack of impulse control. In many instances, they are egocentric individuals who want the world to revolve around them. They prefer to be the hub and others are supposed to do their bidding. Many of them are much like three- or four-year-old children who throw temper tantrums. They want their own way when they want it, where they want it, and how they want it. In other words, they simply want to do the things they want to do regardless of the consequences to others.

No. 2—A normal person can see the difference between socially acceptable and socially unacceptable goals. The implication here is that once the person sees the difference he knows what to do. In other words, he can act on it. The alcoholic, however, for the most part knows the difference between socially acceptable and unacceptable goals but because he is an egocentric individual and wants everything to revolve around him he feels that he doesn't have to be influenced by what others say. There is a strong resistance to authority.

No. 3—A normal person usually selects goals within his grasp. The obvious way to achieve goals is to take one step at a time like climbing a staircase. But there are some personality types in alcoholism which try to skip steps and do too much at one time. The alcoholic, because he does lack impulse control, is impatient. He doesn't want to wait for things to happen, and in some instances he wishes to make them happen. He goes too fast. Because the alcoholic attempts to gain his goals too quickly the stress becomes too great, the pain intolerable, and he reverts to drinking as a form of escape.

No. 4—Normal people learn to vary their behavior. There are infinite ways to handle any problem. The only limitations are those which are self-imposed. One individual has indicated that we human beings never have problems—only opportunities—so basically it depends on how we look at things. A key word is "flexibility." We have to be able to move in different directions to solve problems. Any time only one approach is considered it's going to result in rigid, stereotyped behavior which becomes predictable. Such is the case in alcoholism. The individual has basically one answer to any stress situation—drinking. Variability of behavior allows the individual some creativeness in the method of which he handles his life.

No. 5—A normal person can learn to accept substitute goals if the one he is after is unattainable. When I was at the University of North Dakota there was a student who wanted to become a medical doctor. He had an I.Q. of 100, making it realistically impossible for him to be an M.D. We tried to get him to change his goal and to plan to become a medical technician. He refused, and consequently flunked out of the university. We received an angry letter from him claiming discrimination. He was certain that only sons of medical doctors were allowed to continue the medical program at the university. He went to several other schools where the same thing happened. At last report, this individual had ended up in a state hospital for treatment because he could not attain the goal he had set. He had to find other means of behavior to justify his failure. It was much easier to point to the university and the other schools as the causes for his failure than to accept the blame himself.

No. 6—A normal person learns to satisfy his needs on a reality level. He can distort reality, he can hide from it, he can do anything he wants to with it, but as soon as he opens his eyes again reality is there. There is no way that he can escape from it, so the best thing to do is to work with it. The difficult process is to determine what is reality for oneself. For patients at Valley Hope the reality is that they are in treatment for alcoholism and that there are certain things they have to do if there is to be a recovery program.

No. 7—The normal person learns to tolerate a certain amount of frustration, anxiety, and pain. This is a very important part of being "normal." We all have to learn to accept the ups and downs in our lives. They are going to come regardless of what we do, and the best method of attack is a good offense. We need to be ready to handle these problems as they occur, then not one of them can be the "last straw." People often state that it's the last straw that breaks the camel's back. I prefer to think it's the first straw that breaks the camel's back because without the straw piling up the weight could not be excessive and the individual might be able to handle it. A mother of a mongoloid child indicated that she had been to more than a hundred physicians trying to get one of them to tell her that her daughter was normal. The child's tested I.Q. was 72 which meant that she was trainable and could function quite well at several types of unskilled jobs. The mother, however, wouldn't accept this assessment and insisted that her child was normal. The stress this placed on the child was obvious. She was unable to handle it and began showing signs of emotional disturbance. The mother had very similar types of symptoms. She could not attain her goal. It was like constantly hitting her head against a "brick wall." The strong feelings of negativism which she held toward the medical profession were obviously defensive structures which allowed her to justify her feelings about her child.

No. 8—A normal person is able to satisfy his needs often enough and adequately enough to be able to report to himself that he is happy. Any day he can report 50 percent plus in the positive direction, he has had a good day. The problem is that he doesn't want to accept just 50 percent happiness. He wants to have his cake and to eat it too. I don't believe a person can be 100 percent happy. A day of 70 percent happiness would be an excellent day. There must be ups and downs in a "normal" adjustment pattern.

Step 10 of Alcoholics Anonymous suggests a continued personal inventory. You can go back over the day, find out where your happiness came from, and improve on that. Then determine where your unhappiness came from and do something about that. This also makes an excellent reality check. It might surprise you to find the day, for the most part, much more positive than negative. Humans have a tendency to dwell more on the things that hurt than on the things that please. Try this and see what you come up with.

There are obviously many other facets of a so-called normal adjustment. But if what I'm saying is valid, then there's no reason why an individual who is operating under a tension cannot find a positive form of behavior to relieve that tension. This can be done just as easily as finding a negative form. Part of the difficulty is that thinking becomes routine, rigid, and stereotyped. Insufficient energy is expended on finding creative methods for facing problems.

CHAPTER SEVEN

Creative Thinking (A Means to Problem Solving)

Psychiatry concentrates on thinking more than any other aspect of human behavior. People in the humanities are also greatly concerned with how a person thinks, what is going on in his or her mind.

Human beings have a tendency to allow their thinking to get into a rut. They set up habit patterns which prohibit a great deal of variation. Think for a moment. How do you drive to work? Do you take the same route each day? Most people do. What do you see as you drive to work? Have you ever gone through a stoplight and wondered afterwards if it were red or green? If you repeat the same patterns of behavior over and over you soon begin to be quite unaware of your surroundings. There has to be something out of the ordinary, perhaps a car accident, before you sit up and take notice. This is real rigidity, the repeating of behavior patterns.

In my estimation addictive people are very rigid people. In fact, the alcoholic's behavioral pattern becomes so rigid that accurate predictions can be made regarding the progressive steps of alcoholism.

Why do some choose rigidity? It's fairly easy to

answer. Let's assume that each of us has two worlds. One is the world of reality, the world we live in each day and must adjust to if we are going to be "normal" people. We all have problems and there is no way we will ever be free from problems unless one considers death as freedom. It is the way we deal with our problems that determines whether we are adjusted or maladjusted. If we have a good grasp on the real world, then as each problem comes up we deal with it as quickly as possible. By so doing we allow ourselves a continual flow of mental energy to handle the problems.

Say, for instance, that the meat packing plant where you have worked for many years is closing down. You have no control over the closing of the plant yet you do have control over your action regarding the closing. If you are living in the real world you accept the closing of the plant and begin to formulate an action plan. This plan will obviously include another job. You begin to search. You find that beef slaughterers are not in great demand, so you change your direction and look for a job commensurate with your other talents. Perhaps you take training in other occupations and find your job that way. You do not allow the stress of the loss of a job to "throw" you. Rather you accept it then formulate appropriate plans to handle the problem. This is adjustment to your real world.

Let's look at a different approach to the same problem. Assume you lose your job after several years of loyalty to the company. You begin to build up resentments which in turn produce feelings of helplessness which make you an angry person. You begin fighting the company, writing letters, talking to management, but to no avail. You take each rejection personally. Your anger increases and you say they can't do this to you, and by heaven, they are not going to get away with it. You will fight to the very end. You will show them. All your thoughts are concentrated on the idea that you deserve better treatment from the company and you are going to get it. All you can think about are the injustices done to you. Your main thrust in life has become to change injustice to justice. Whether you like it or not at this stage you have become a rigid person. Whether you succeed or not in your quest for justice is not an issue here. But once you have placed yourself in the position in which you allow yourself only one goal (to get rid of the injustice) then your life must now revolve around this goal.

An example is the man who buys an expensive camper. To justify the expense, all vacations must center around the camper. He concedes that he can go many places but considers only one way to get there—in the camper.

We tend to get lazy in our thinking and take the easy route of habit thinking. When we repeat the same detrimental behavior over and over we're in trouble. Then it's imperative to switch gears and try something new!

What is thinking? The dictionary defines it as exercising the mental capacities, mental action, or thought. I'm going to give you a command and I want you to respond, but more importantly, I want you to try to determine where the response comes from. Okay—think of a vegetable.

What did you come up with? Most patients at Valley Hope say carrot, peas, radish, onion, etcetera.

They have an easy time giving me the name of a vegetable, but a difficult time telling me how it arrived in their minds. It's really not difficult. The word you came up with is due to an experience you have had in your life. You associated the name of a vegetable with the stimulus command I gave you. There could be many reasons why you thought of the vegetable but they all boil down to the fact that you had to experience the vegetable somewhere in your past. Thinking then is made up of past associations, pleasant or unpleasant. This is a simple explanation but one that suffices.

It takes energy to think; in fact, at times it's downright hard work. Any man who uses brain power in his job will tell you how tired he is after a day at work. Perhaps this is one of the reasons why we become rigid, especially in our thinking. Once the behavior becomes a set pattern we need not "think" about it but can repeat our behavior on the basis of habit.

To determine whether or not your thinking has become rigid, try the nine dot problem. It is a simple arrangement of dots which looks like this:

• • •

• • •

• • •

Copy these nine dots on a separate sheet of paper. Then with four straight lines connect each dot without lifting your pencil or retracing. Take about two minutes. . . .

Most people do not solve this problem because their minds close the dots into a square. As long as they think square the problem cannot be solved. Now try getting out of the square; take a few more minutes to solve this but *get out of the square.* . . . Let me help you:

The result above is termed creative thinking. You had to leave the square, you had to change your way of looking at the dots, and you knew this; yet most of you couldn't solve this problem. Why? Simply because you have allowed your thinking to become rigid and you couldn't vary your behavior.

Creative thinking is much more than just thinking. It really is designed as problem-solving behavior. In essence, it allows a change of gears in the mind and presents the same old problem in new prospective. The only thing limiting a person in problem-solving behavior is the person. Creative thinking allows a change in thought patterns and gives the individual new ways of approaching old problems. An individual who has only one outlet for his behavior will find his life-style centered around that outlet. The alcoholic handles his life with the continual use of alcohol even when he knows he will be in serious trouble as a result.

In order to acquire a varied approach to problem solving, there needs to be some creativity. Two beautiful young women utilized this approach to a problem they faced. They wanted to spend their Christmas holidays in Colorado at a ski resort. The problem—no money. They began "thinking." The end result—they decided to advertise their services as housecleaners. They were soon swamped with offers and they not only made enough money to go to Colorado but made enough to take a friend. Where was the creativity? The advertising read that they would clean only bachelor apartments and their uniforms were "bunny suits." Now that was a new approach to an old problem.

What's necessary for one to change his thinking? Well, just as for a good cook, there is a recipe. First, there must be a problem. That is the easiest part; we all have problems. They may vary from individual to individual but a problem is a problem. Pick one specifically as you "think" through this recipe.

Second, there must be no limitations placed on finding a solution to that problem. I know of a man who is sober today because of the no limitations concept. He had an overpowering urge to drink at one point in his life and was becoming fearful that he wasn't going to be able to maintain his sobriety. Knowing the consequences of commencing to drink he walked up to a police officer, told him he was an alcoholic, and asked to spend the night in jail. The officer was a little taken aback but told this man that he hadn't broken the law so he couldn't arrest him. The alcoholic promptly hit the officer and was marched off to jail. Results—he didn't drink, he strengthened his sobriety by this, and the officer had a heart and didn't charge him with the offense. Some might say, "Man, what a nut—hitting a policeman."

Think a moment about what this alcoholic was really saying: "My sobriety is more important to me than going to jail." He found a way to preserve it. No doubt there would have been other solutions to his problem but his feeling level at that time made this solution acceptable to him.

Third, strive for some originality. Actually, nothing is truly original. We review our knowledge and past experiences, rearrange them and alter them to fit the present situation, and say we come up with a new idea. Then we try out the new idea to see if it works. Take the hula hoop for example. There was nothing really new about a hoop; the designers simply suggested a different use for it and had the ability to sell the idea. I was talking to a student about graduate school. He indicated that he was fearful of going because one of the requirements of the Ph.D. program was to add something new to the knowledge of the world. He didn't think he could do that. Most people are afraid to try what to them is the unknown, yet there are many more things that are unknown than are known. There is a paucity of knowledge in the field of alcoholism for instance. Many people could spend a lifetime on "original" research in this field alone.

The fourth step to creativity is all that's necessary to make originality possible: be flexible. This is where many of us fail. We become accustomed to one form of behavior and if it works well we continue to use it. I ask the alcoholics sitting in a lecture at Valley Hope how many different ways there are to get to the blackboard in the front of the room. The usual answer is to get up, go down the aisle, and approach the board. When I press for more answers it takes awhile before they realize that one can run, crawl, walk backwards, hop, skip, as well as approach from different directions, or remove obstacles such as the chairs in front of them. If you're having trouble with problems I might suggest that you give flexibility top billing in your life.

Fifth, you must want a solution. Motivation becomes an important aspect of creativity. No matter how much energy we use to get an alcoholic to look at himself, in the final analysis *he* has to put it all together and then use it as a part of *his* life. Reams have been written about motivation. The key question is still "Do you want a solution?" Your answer determines what you will or will not do with the limits of your capabilities. One can't always do everything because of limitations. A mentally retarded person cannot be a bank president but he can do the best he is able to do with his assets. He can perform in some avenue of life.

You now have the ingredients for creative thinking: a problem, no limits on solutions, originality, flexibility, and motivation.

In spite of the fact that you now have this knowledge about how to be creative, chances are that you will still remain "in the square." Since a problem is the necessary first step in creative thinking, I'm going to give you a problem. Before I do, however, would you get a piece of paper and pencil? I want you to write down your answers to the problem as creatively as you can. The problem: I have an empty three-pound can with a lid. What can be done with this coffee can? Stop reading here and write down your answers, then come on back and read some more....

Some of the more common answers that have been given are the following: use for cookie can, to hold nuts and bolts, cut out bottom and use for covering tomato plants, worm can, paint can, cannister set, odds-and-ends can, put dirty oil in it, and on and on. Look at these answers. Is your answer limited as they are by the shape of the three-pound coffee can? All of the above are limited, and it is this limitation that places them in the "square" (even if the can is round). Come on, get out of the square.

Next—what is this?

Most of you said to yourselves, "A triangle." You are *wrong*. It's not a triangle until the ends meet. It's actually three straight lines in the shape of a triangle; but according to your past experiences anything in that shape is a triangle. Your mind closed the edges. I'm suggesting that you need to keep an open mind, a flexible mind, and that you use your brain power in this new way. It's fun to think and it's fun to think creatively. Get out of the "square." Use your brain power. The good Lord gave it to you to use. There are thousands of areas of your life that you could look at creatively and find much more enjoyable as a result. A few suggestions—lawn mowing, fence mending, painting, dishwashing, cooking, house-cleaning, hobbies, work, church, and literally any aspect of your life that you want to enhance by creativeness.

Creativeness takes a little more energy but the results are well worth it. Just for practice sit down and think of the part of your life that's most boring to you. Now think of new ways of approaching it. Then comes the most important part: put the new way or ways you like best into *action*. Remember, "the road to hell is paved with good intentions." If you are going to benefit from this concept of "getting out of the square" you're going to have to put the advice into an action plan. As we tell the alcoholics at Valley Hope, "Get off your duffs and get going!"

CHAPTER EIGHT

Responsibility

From creative thinking to responsibility—that is a big transition for anyone, yet I suspect that you can approach the transition more creatively now. One of the major problems seen in alcoholism is the alcoholic's uncanny ability to escape responsibility for his actions. The following scene is repeated in many homes on Monday morning following "the night before."

Fred, yelling from the bedroom: "Mary, Mary get in here." Mary arrives and Fred states, "I feel rotten. I'm sick. Call the boss and tell him I'm sick. I can't go to work feeling like this. Please call. I don't want to lose my job." Mary doesn't want him to lose his job either so she makes the call. It's another case of Monday morning "flu," one to be repeated many more times if Mary continues to assume Fred's responsibilities.

Let's break this scene down so we can understand it. Fred feels terrible. There is no doubt that he is "under the weather," although it might be more appropriate to say "under the booze." He is feeling sick and he is concerned about the job. Mary is also concerned about the job because it brings in the funds for living. She calls for him when he asks as it seems the logical thing to do. Fred's problem comes about because of the drinking the night before when he consumed too much. Mary's willingness to assume what should be Fred's responsibility allows Fred the privilege of getting off the hook. He can fall back into bed having suffered no consequences of his drinking behavior other than that he feels lousy. With the use of a few defense mechanisms such as rationalization he can justify the whole event. By lying to the boss Mary has, in effect, granted Fred permission to continue with his drinking.

The dictionary defines responsibility as "the state of being responsible or accountable; that for which one is answerable, a duty or a trust; ability to meet obligations or to act without superior authority or guidance." Suppose we were to declare that no one on this planet had to be responsible. Take a few minutes before reading on and try to imagine what life would be like. Write down words that would describe this condition.

The word that shows up most often at Valley Hope when I ask this question is "chaos." It's probably the best word. If all of us could do whatever we wanted to do with no consequences for our behavior we would certainly live in a world of utter chaos. When the practicing alcoholic loses the ability to be responsible for his own behavior, his world becomes chaotic, too. As responsibility for behavior diminishes, problems become greater. If one cannot accept responsibility then one must find others to be responsible for him. In most instances the alcoholic must find someone who loves him very much, for I assure you no one else would put up with the immature behavior of such an irresponsible person.

The alcoholic literally shuns responsible behavior. He, of course, would be the last one to admit it. One needs only to look at a few areas of his life to determine the lack of responsible behavior. Ask the family of a practicing alcoholic if he is responsible. It won't take long for smoldering resentments to surface. Take neglect of his job. I've heard any number of alcoholics state that their drinking has never interfered with their work. Of course from their point of view it hasn't, but really can one be as efficient with a hangover as without one? Neglect of self is another area of irresponsibility. One doesn't have to look too far to see this. The physiological damage inflicted by the disease is apparent but when damage to self-respect is added to that the result of irresponsibility toward oneself can readily be seen.

How does irresponsible behavior come about? It doesn't just happen. There are reasons for it. Diagrams of situations may be helpful in understanding relationships to (1) the real world and (2) the problem world.

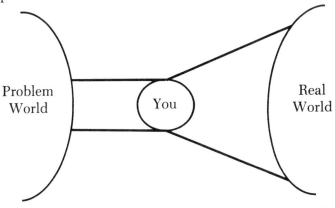

Problem World   You   Real World

If you have a good grasp on the real world and a small outlet to your problem world it means that your behavior is considered "normal." As problems come up you handle them. This means there can be no "last straw that broke the camel's back" because you don't allow the straws to accumulate. You take care of each problem as it emerges.

There are individuals who have a large grasp on their problem world and only a small grasp on the real world. These include alcoholics, drug addicts, persons in an anxiety state, depressed persons, and others. Most of their mental energies have to be expended on problems. There is very little energy left to handle the real world. This means that the behavior in the real world becomes rigid and stereotyped.

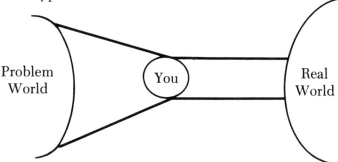

The alcoholic is a superb example of this, for the disease of alcoholism is predictable in terms of an alcoholic's behavior pattern. As an individual becomes more and more irresponsible—in other words, as the problem world builds—the real world that the irresponsible person has to live in shrinks. If there is enough shrinkage then the behavior becomes predictable and others can put a diagnostic label on the behavior. It was said before that in chronic stages the alcoholic lives to drink and drinks to live. His life centers around the consumption of alcohol. He becomes the slave mentioned in Chapter One. The problem becomes the lord and master and the individual must model his life after the problem.

As the alcoholism progresses the alcoholic must find ways to rid himself of the label of irresponsibility. No one is going to go around telling himself openly that he is an immature, irresponsible person, so there has to be a defense. Blane states that the alcoholic is in a constant state of rage. I feel that it is the alcoholic's anger that allows him to control others. It is this anger that others respond to usually in an angry way. Remember Fred and Mary and the fight that resulted from the angry response? The alcoholic needs the angry response of others to continue his own behavior.

Anxiety is another method used by the alcoholic to handle people. A classic example of this was a twenty-nine-year-old married alcoholic father of several children who had the bad habit of writing insufficient fund checks. Merchants became a little perturbed with these checks and began turning them over to the authorities. Whenever the young man got into trouble he would pick up the phone and call his mother. She would hurry down and pay off the checks, receiving her son's solemn word that he would never do that again. Literally all Mom was doing was giving her son permission to write another insufficient funds check. When this alcoholic was brought into treatment we tried very hard to explain the game the son was playing. The mother's response was denial and "There will never be any shame on our family name as long as I live." The game would continue because the alcoholic had Mom operating under the pain of the anxiety engendered in her by the behavior of her son. She relieved the anxiety by paying the checks. She did tell us about all the hurt she was going through, but she could never quite lay her finger on the cause of the hurt within her. To make a long story short, the son took the parents for everything they had. Perhaps we should say the mother allowed the son to take everything they had. Both acted in an irresponsible way.

Valley Hope's program is geared toward a person accepting responsibility for his actions. I feel strongly that unless this is accomplished the alcoholic will continue drinking to resolve his problems. How does one go about achieving responsible behavior? I'd like to share with you two stories which I think answer this question. These stories take place in New England in the 1700's. It is late fall.

HOW TO SLEEP ON A WINDY NIGHT

The squire's handyman had just left him and he had to find another man to work on his farm. He hitched up the buggy and drove to town to find help. He interviewed several people, none of whom were too impressive, but finally chose John because he had to find help that day for the farm. They returned to the farm and the squire tried to teach John about how he wanted the work done. Before he could show John everything the squire was called away on business. He was gone three days. On his way home a terrible New England squall came up with high winds and heavy rains. The squire became very fearful that the storm would endanger his cattle, sheep, and particularly the winter's supply of hay. He whipped his horse and hurried home.

He arrived at the farm, dashed from the buggy to the house, lit a lantern, and ran to the barn. Lo and behold, the barn was shuttered and the door closed. The squire opened the barn door and there were the cattle munching on the hay that John had given them. The squire was relieved but then thought of the sheep. He raced around the barn and there found his sheep huddled together safe and sound. Then he thought of his hay and hurried to the field where the haystacks were all covered and weighted down to protect them from the wind. The squire stood there cold and wet, becoming quite angry at himself for having been so worried. As he went back to the house there was lightning and thunder all about him, so he hurriedly entered through the back door. John's bedroom door was partly open and the squire looked in. John was sleeping soundly, snoring to high heaven. The squire thought, John has taught me a lesson I hope I never forget. He has taught me how to sleep on a windy night!

There is a beautiful moral here. John could sleep because he was at peace with himself. He had accomplished all his tasks in a responsible manner and could sleep through the storm. How about the storms in your life? Are they handled responsibly or irresponsibly?

HOW TO GET A CAT OUT OF THE CUPBOARD WITHOUT BREAKING THE DISHES

In the kitchen of the squire's house next to the fireplace was a large cupboard with a broken latch. The squire's cat loved to climb into the cupboard and sleep in the warmth of the heat reflecting off the glass cupboard doors. Every time the squire walked into the kitchen and saw his cat in the cupboard he became very upset because he knew his wife didn't approve of this at all. He would run across the room yelling at the cat. Of course the old cat would be frightened and leap out of the cupboard bringing several dishes crashing to the floor. One day John was with the squire when they noticed the cat in the cupboard. The squire started yelling again, but John asked him to stop. John, seemingly ignoring the cat, got a saucer of cream and put it on the floor. The old cat looked at the cream, stretched a bit, and gingerly stepped over the dishes, not breaking a one as he jumped down to get his meal. The squire stood there in amazement. "Not only has John taught me how to sleep on a windy night," he said, "but now he's taught me how to get a cat out of the cupboard without breaking the dishes!"

One of the main tenets of responsible behavior illustrated by the story is "think before you act." Often the alcoholic is an impulsive person who acts before he thinks. The responsible person considers the consequences of his actions before he carries them out. Which way would you choose? Perhaps this is why there are often signs that read "Think Think Think" in an A.A. meeting room.

None of us are responsible for everything that happens to us. For instance, we can't control the weather. A tornado or a flood could wipe us out. However, we are responsible for the way we act when things happen to us. We can fall to pieces, curse our lives, and let our resentments and hatred toward a situation or person take over our lives. Or we can find constructive means of handling our problems. We can consider problems as opportunities, opportunities to grow. God doesn't give us more than we can bear; we may think he does but really he doesn't. If we treat our problems as opportunities, life can and will be better. Responsible behavior will allow us the opportunity to grow. Irresponsibility can only bring the world down on our shoulders. I don't have the strength to hold the world up. Do you?

CHAPTER NINE

Why Do I Have to Be Me?

Why do I have to be me? You don't. You can build facades to hide your real self. Perhaps the question should be, "Why can't I be the real me?" Most of us hide behind a facade at one time or another. Our table manners get better away from home; we act differently in a crowd of strangers than we do with our friends; we dress differently at home than we do when we go away. We behave differently under different settings. Why?

We act as we do to secure certain satisfactions in our lives. We do things and behave in ways that allow us to feel content with ourselves or to look good to others.

We all have needs. There is something lacking in all of us. We try to offset that lack so that we present a positive appearance to ourselves and to others.

We have physical and psychological needs. When these needs are out of balance our bodies inform us that it's time to do something to bring back a sense of balance. If we are hungry we eat, if we are thirsty we drink, if we are warm we try to cool ourselves, and if we are cold we try to warm ourselves.

A scientific analysis shows us what happens. We find ourselves under tension; when the tension goes up we receive feelings of uncomfortableness which in turn motivate us to a behavioral adjustment. Thus, HUNGER (TENSION) = EATING (BEHAVIORAL ADJUSTMENT) which results in reduced hunger (comfortable feelings).

It's easy to understand our physical needs, but not so easy to understand our psychological needs. However, the mind must also be in balance. When that balance is lost, an attempt is made to find means which will give us the sense of psychological balance. For instance, many alcoholics have a very difficult time expressing themselves in group settings. This creates tension, a feeling of uncomfortableness. This uncomfortableness motivates the alcoholic to take several drinks, after which he finds he can converse with his peers. The sedative effect of the alcohol reduces the tension of his inner feelings and for a period of time the alcoholic functions "normally." I believe it is this desire for "normalcy" that motivates much of the tension-reducing behavior we see, not only in alcoholics but in many other types of mental illness.

It is perfectly reasonable for a person who has found an adequate adjustment to stress not to want to give up that behavior just because someone requests it. This is important for those of us dealing with the alcoholic to understand. It is particularly crucial that spouses of alcoholics comprehend it. The alcoholic has found a method of adjusting to his stress, a method that works beautifully. His adjustment method allows him freedom to behave normally. He is not aware of the pain (stress) he inflicts on others.

When their pain becomes so great and they ask him to change his adjustment he must answer *"NO!"*

True, he says he will stop. He promises many things but he cannot deliver them, for if he gives up his adjustment he is literally catapulting himself into chaos and loss of security. This he will not do. Neither would anyone else.

Charles Schultz's "Peanuts" character Linus needs a blanket for his security. Take away his blanket and he literally falls to pieces. When Grandma comes to visit, Linus schemes to keep her from getting his blanket. He must, for the essence of comfortableness is derived from his security blanket. Like Linus, the alcoholic falls apart when asked for his security blanket, his bottle. He wants to give it up, yet he just can't because to do so would jeopardize his "normalcy." So he makes excuses and defenses.

The secret is to ask for the alcohol but to give him something in return, something to fill the void created by the loss of a solution to a problem. Alcoholics Anonymous does this beautifully. It literally gives the alcoholic a new way of life in trade for his alcohol. A.A.'s fellowship, the reaching of the hand in help, the sharing of experience, and the almost total giving of oneself to another suffering alcoholic replaces the alcohol with the greatest single gift one has to give—love of one's fellows.

While it is true that TENSION + ALCOHOL = REDUCED TENSION, it might just as well be TENSION + A.A. = REDUCED TENSION.

A.A. suggests the development of an action program. If the same amount of mental energy is put into a recovery program that is invested in active alcoholism there should be success.

Every person's battle in life is the battle for personal worth. He wants to be acceptable to himself and to those he loves. He needs help to see the goodness which is in all people. But he particularly needs to feel that he is a worthwhile person.

Maslow indicates that human needs can be categorized into five areas—physical, security, love, esteem, and self-actualization.

We have already touched on the urgency of responding to our physical needs. There can be no survival if these hunger-thirst-warmth needs are ignored. There are tribes in Africa, for instance, that spend all of their waking moments searching for food. Needless to say, they are not so concerned with satisfying other needs until their physical needs are cared for.

The need for safety or security is the next concern. The individual strives for an understanding that his basic needs will continue to be met and then he launches out to discover what his comfortable limitations are. There is security in being able to operate within these limitations.

With the survival needs and safety needs met, Maslow claims humans are next motivated to seek for a sense of belonging. This is the need for love. It involves not only the capacity to be loved but also to love others. To give love assumes a risk, a risk that others will not receive it and then we will be hurt and rejected. The fear of rejection from others stops us from risking. This is one of the situations where the defense of withdrawal comes into play. The tendency is to avoid the risk situation, the source of possible injury, and to seek a comfortable situation.

Yet we need to know that we belong, that we are a

part of things in life. As we mature we become willing to risk rejection and still offer love. At Valley Hope love is defined as the giving of oneself without expectation of reward; the reaching out for others simply because we want to, not because we have to. An A.A. member goes out to help a practicing alcoholic. This is risking. There is certainly the possibility that he will be rejected by the practicing alcoholic. Yet the A.A. member has found an inner peace, and to keep it he gives it away. He risks and the rewards can be great.

Basically we humans are very selfish people. We want other people to recognize us, to do things for us. We will even reach out to do things for them as long as they give us the appropriate recognition for what we're doing. What is hard is to learn to love a person for what he is, not what you desire him to be. This does not mean that inappropriate behavior must be accepted, but rather that love is given even to the person who is behaving inappropriately.

The fourth level is the need for esteem. This is what I'm suggesting the whole battle for life is all about—learning to develop a healthy sense of personal worth. We need to experience some degree of success and to be able to respect ourselves. That is why it is so important to concentrate on short spans of time during difficult periods of one's life. The A.A. day-at-a-time theory allows one to achieve success daily and thus reinforces an often sagging self-image. I think it vitally interesting that the need for love comes before the need for self-esteem. Perhaps that is why it is so difficult, if not impossible, for us to give of ourselves in love to others and still feel self-derogatory. Discovering and appreciating selfhood is a vital step in human development.

Satisfaction of the other needs allows one to concentrate on the need for self-actualization. This refers to the need to develop the full potentialities of the person. Naturally the meaning of this need varies from person to person, for each has different potentialities. For some, it means achievement in literary or scientific fields; for others, it means leadership in politics or the community; for still others, it means merely living one's own life fully without being unduly restrained by social conventions. One can find "self-actualizers" among professors, businessmen, political leaders, missionaries, artists, or housewives. But not all individuals in any of these categories are able to achieve self-actualization; many have numerous unsatisfied needs, and because their achievements are merely compensations, they are left frustrated and unhappy in other respects.

I can suggest to you without too much fear of contradiction that once you find the inner peace accompanying a feeling of personal worth by giving your love to your fellows, you are going to become a self-actualized person.

> I sought my soul,
>> But my soul I could not see.
> I sought my God,
>> But my God eluded me.
> I sought my brother—
>> And I found all three.

> —Author Unknown

Selected Bibliography

1. *Alcoholics Anonymous*, New York, Alcoholics Anonymous World Services, Inc., 1955.
2. *Alcoholics Anonymous Comes of Age*, New York, Alcoholics Anonymous World Services, Inc., 1957.
3. Blane, Howard T., Ph.D., *The Personality of the Alcoholic—Guises of Dependency*, New York: Harper & Row, 1968.
4. Clinebell, Reverend H. J., Jr., *Understanding and Counseling the Alcoholic*, Nashville: Abingdon Press, 1956.
5. *Funk & Wagnalls Standard College Dictionary*, New York: Funk & Wagnalls, A Division of Reader's Digest Books, Inc., 1968.
6. Guthrie, E. R., *The Psychology of Learning*, New York: Harper & Row, viii, 1935, pp. 3-247.
7. Lewin, K., *A Dynamic Theory of Personality*, New York: McGraw-Hill, 1935.
8. *Living with an Alcoholic*, New York: Al-Anon Family Group Headquarters, Inc., 1971.
9. Mann, Marty, *New Primer on Alcoholism*, New York: Holt, Rinehart & Winston, 1958, p. 66.
10. Maslow, A. H., "A Theory of Human Motivation," *Psychological Review*, L1943.
11. Peter, Dr. Laurence J., and Hull, Raymond, *The Peter Principle—Why Things Always Go Wrong*, New York: New York: Bantam Books, Wm. Morrow & Co., Inc., 1969.

12. Skinner, B. F., *The Behavior of Organisms*, New York: Appleton-Century-Crofts, 1938.
13. *The Dilemma of the Alcoholic Marriage*, New York, Al-Anon Family Group Headquarters, Inc., 1971.
14. Tournier, Paul, *To Understand Each Other*, Richmond, Virginia: John Knox Press, 1972, 12th printing, translated by John S. Gilmour from "Difficultes conjugales," Geneva, Switzerland: Editions Labor et Fides, 1962.
15. Whaley, Donald, and Malott, Richard, *Elementary Principles of Behavior*, New York: Appleton-Century-Crofts, 1971.